FIX YOUR FOCUS

BETH SCHREIBER

Trilogy Christian Publishers
A Wholly Owned Subsidary of Trinity Broadcasting Network
2442 Michelle Drive
Tustin, CA 92780

Cover design by: Cornerstone Creative Solutions

For information, address Trilogy Christian Publishing
Rights Department, 2442 Michelle Drive, Tustin, Ca 92780.
Trilogy Christian Publishing/ TBN and colophon are trademarks of Trinity
Broadcasting Network.

For information about special discounts for bulk purchases, please contact
Trilogy Christian Publishing.

Manufactured in the United States of America

10 9 8 7 6 5 4 3 2 1

Library of Congress Cataloging-in-Publication Data is available.

ISBN 978-1-63769-280-6 (Print Book)
ISBN 978-1-63769-281-3 (ebook)

Is your life "out of focus?" Are your days full of joy and peace or are they full of stress and chaos? Do you experience more "I can't live like this" moments than you would care to admit?

Many people think that there is no "real peace" in this life that they are living, that it is almost to the point of feeling like tomorrow will probably be worse than today; you know that old mentality of "what else can go wrong?" Worry, anxiousness, hopelessness, sadness, dread, fear, depression. This list can go on and on, so, what is the answer? How can you get past this? Is there a way?

Good news, yes! It can be done! I know you are probably saying, "Yeah, we know, Jesus is the answer. Blah, blah, blah. Heard this sermon already, maybe even several sermons, But I am *still* feeling overwhelmed!"

I get it. And yes, I am here to say that *Jesus is the way*. So, to get started on this journey, we need to get our priorities straight. Hopefully, by the time you get to the end of this book, you will have a few new tools in your "spiritual tool belt" to help build a better life!

TABLE OF CONTENTS

CHAPTER 1

....

Identifying Who You Really Are

Identity. This is so important! Who are you? I know you might say, "Jane from Wyoming, I am 5'2 with brown hair. I am a divorced, mother of one, secretary, I love hiking, swimming, and eating pizza, I love comedies, hate horror films, and enjoy a nice lazy day in front of the television occasionally."

Okay, this sounds like part of an online dating profile, but this is usually how people respond when you ask them that question. Nothing is wrong with this answer, it is just missing a few key ingredients to the completeness of who you really are. For instance, if I were to ask you about your fears, your doubts, or your concerns, would you answer sincerely or lightly brush it off? Would the truth contain that you are so worried about finances that you have a hard time sleeping at night, or that you are so stressed about your health that it is literally making you sick? Would you say that you are a "worry wart" or that you feel so overwhelmed sometimes that you almost are in a state of panic?

Many times, people are so bound up in a life of self-hatred, they have low self-esteem or have a life of feeling like you are never enough or never good enough, not smart enough, pretty enough, have low self-worth, or an actual belief that nothing good could ever happen to you. You know that old saying "If you never get your hopes up, you can never be disappointed." That unfortunately, can become a way of life for a lot of folks. Seems like a pretty depressing way to exist, but for some, it just "is what it is."

Sometimes, circumstances of life have kept us bound up in this seemingly never-ending cycle of this kind of thought pattern. Society says that we must act or look a certain way, family and friends say we must always be a certain way and sometimes the expectation of others is almost unreasonable. Then you have the guilt of not being what they expect or not doing what they expect and on top of that, not knowing how to do or be these things. So, what can help, what do we need to do to turn this thing around?

Does it seem that you are constantly trying to 'chase" an idea or an image that you long to be or that someone expects you to be? Are you chasing the desires of your flesh or are you seeking to bring God into your daily routine and into every area of your life? Are you seeking identity in something other than God?

It is so easy to be crushed by failures or weaknesses. So easy to get caught up in pride over a successful career or a hefty bank account, or to fall into despair over a loss or maybe getting looked over for a promotion, or easily getting caught up in guilt over things that may not even be in your ability to control, making poor decisions, etc. This could really turn into a long list. I know people that are so fearful and anxious about the future that they are just an emotional wreck.

You may ask, what does worry have to do with identity? A lot. If you knew that God only wanted the best for you and has actually promised this, that revelation would be a game changer! If you were solid in that knowledge, it would change how you viewed life.

Wouldn't it be great if we had no need to judge or compare ourselves to others? Imagine that! Do you identify yourself by a personality trait, your career or profession, or this one is huge, an illness or disease? How many times have you heard a conversation or been part of a conversation that revolved around the person that is sick? Example "Oh, yes, I am diabetic" or, "I am bipolar." Does it seem like the person is just immersed in that label? It is so unfortunate that a person cannot seem to "be" anything other than what society has labeled them. It is so easy to fall into this lifestyle because it seems to be an ever-present situation that appears to be never ending and hopeless.

So where is the answer or what is the answer? First, we need to go to the source! What is that? The source is the One who created you! We need to explore the Word of God and find out what He says!

Let us start with a list of what God says about us:

1. I am the head, and not the tail; always above and not beneath,
   (Adapted from Deuteronomy 28:13, AMPC)

2. I am fearfully and wonderfully made.
   (Psalms 139:14-15, KJV)

3. I am healed and whole because of Calvary
   (Adapted from Isaiah 53:5 and 1 Peter 2:24, AMPC)

4. I am righteous, far from oppression and will not live in fear and terror.
   (Adapted from Isaiah, 54:14 AMPC)

5. I am the light of the world.
   (Adapted from Matthew 5:14, AMPC)

6. I am merciful, sympathetic, tender, responsive, and compassionate, I am forgiving and not judgmental.
   (Adapted from Luke 6:36-37, AMPC)

7. I am a friend of God and I have been chosen by God.
   (Adapted from John 15:15-16, AMPC)

8. I am justified, acquitted, made righteous, and brought into right relationship with God by Christ's blood.
   (Adapted from Rom 5:9, AMPC)

9. 9. I am dead to sin and alive to God and I live in unbroken fellowship with Him in Christ Jesus.
   (Adapted from Rom 6:11, AMPC)

10. I am free.
    (Adapted from Romans 8:2, AMPC)

11. Amid all things I am more than a conqueror and gain a surpassing victory through Him who loves me.
    (Adapted from Romans 8:37, AMPC)

12. 12. I have the mind of Christ, full of Godly attitude and wisdom.
(Adapted from 1 Corinthians 2:6-7 and Philippians 2:5, AMPC)

13. I am a child of God and a joint heir with Christ.
(Adapted from Romans. 8:17, AMPC)

14. My body is the temple (the very sanctuary) of the Holy Spirit who lives within me, this is a Gift from God! I am not my own, I belong to HIM!
(Adapted from 1 Corinthians 6:19-20, AMPC)

15. I am a new creation (a new creature altogether); the old [previous moral and spiritual condition] has passed away. Behold, the fresh and new has come.
(Adapted from 2 Corinthians 5:17, AMPC)

16. I am an ambassador for Christ, and I am approved and accepted and in right relationship with Him, by His goodness.
(Adapted from 2 Corinthians 5:20-21, AMPC)

17. I am redeemed from the curse of the law and its condemnation.
(Adapted from Galatians 3:13, AMPC)

18. I am chosen and holy and I have been adopted as HIS own child.
(Adapted from Ephesians 1:4-5 and 1Peter 1:16, AMPC)

19. I have been redeemed, delivered and have salvation through His blood, and I am forgiven.
(Adapted from Ephesians 1:7, AMPC)

20. I have received a spirit of wisdom and revelation in the knowledge of Him, and my heart has been flooded with light, so that I can know and understand the hope to which He has called me, and how rich is His glorious inheritance for me.
(Adapted from Ephesians 1:17-18, AMPC)

21. I am alive with Christ, in spite of my past shortcomings.
(Adapted from Ephesians 2:5, AMPC)

22. I am God's own handiwork and workmanship, recreated in Christ Jesus, and born anew.
(Adapted from Ephesians 2:10, AMPC)

23. I live my life by faith and extinguish any attack from the enemy.
(Adapted from Ephesians 6:16, AMPC)

24. I am a citizen of Heaven.
(Adapted from Philippians 3:20, AMPC)

25. I have peace that surpasses understanding.
(Adapted from Philippians 4:7, AMPC)

26. I have strength for all things in Christ Who empowers me.
(Adapted from Philippians 4:13, AMPC)

27. God supplies my every need.
    (Adapted from Philippians 4:19, AMPC)

28. I have strength and power because of His mighty glory,
    (Adapted from Colossians 1:11, AMPC)

29. I have been delivered from darkness and have been transferred into HIS kingdom! God has drawn me to Himself!
    (Adapted from Colossians 1:13, AMPC)

30. I am complete in Him who is that head of all rule and authority.
    (Adapted from Colossians 2:10, AMPC)

31. I am chosen and handpicked by God.
    (Adapted from Colossians 3:12, AMPC)

32. I am clothed with a new nature and am constantly being renewed in the knowledge of God.
    (Adapted from Colossians 3:9-10, AMPC)

33. I do not live in fear, I am full of power and have a sound mind.
    (Adapted from 2 Timothy 1:7, AMPC)

34. I submit to God and because of this I can resist the devil [stand firm against him], and he flees from me.
    (Adapted from James 4:7, AMPC)

35. I draw near to God and He draws near to me.
(Adapted from James 4:8, AMPC)

36. As I Humble myself in the presence of the Lord, He lifts me up and makes my life significant.
(Adapted from James 4:10, AMPC)

37. I have been born again, I am chosen by God, special and set apart.
(Adapted from 1 Peter 1:23 and 1 Peter 2:9, AMPC)

38. He who lives in me is greater than he who is in the world.
(Adapted from 1 John 4:4, AMPC)

39. I am born of God, protected from evil.
(Adapted from 1 John 5:18, AMPC)

40. I am an overcomer.
(Adapted from Revelation 12:11, AMPC)

Okay, so that was a relatively short list compared to *all* that the Bible says about your identity. That was just a taste of the reality of *who* you really are! So, if you are believing anything contrary to the list, you are mistaken!

It is easy to get wrapped up in wrong thinking about who God says you are. You may have always had a negative view of yourself, your looks, your level of intelligence, your worth and value. Maybe because of bad relationships, family issues; there are a number of reasons that someone may feel a little less than. Sometimes, because of past experiences in life, it is hard to identify with the "truth" of God's Word, but the goal here is to accept the truth and let go of the deceptions that the enemy has thrown your way. The devil is a "thought thrower."

> Ephesians 6:16 (AMPC) Lift up over all the [covering] shield of saving faith, upon which you can quench all the flaming missiles of the wicked [one].

> John 10:10 (AMPC) The thief comes only in order to steal and kill and destroy. I came that they may have and enjoy life, and have it in abundance (to the full, till it overflows).

The devil is out to try to steal your joy and your confidence, he is out to destroy anything that remotely resembles peace. If he can convince you that God's Word does not apply to you, then he thinks he has a chance of keeping you in a state of despair. Some folks are stuck in a huge identity crisis because of this! The problem is, they do not see past his façade… See, he cannot really steal your identity. The only thing that he can do is try to convince you that he can. He thinks he is slick. But this only works if we buy into his lies. He knows that if you do not realize who you *really* are, then when situations arise, and things are going haywire, you will not know where to turn.

The enemy knows and understands that God's Word is true, but his job is to convince you otherwise. He is not doing anything differently than he did in the Garden of Eden when he asked Eve "did God *really* say?" (ref: Genesis 3:1) He likes to make people second guess the truth.

In John 8:44 (AMPC) Jesus states that some of the characteristics of the devil is to convince people to practice the lusts and gratify the desires of the flesh. He was a murderer from the beginning and does not stand in the truth, because there is no truth in him. When he speaks a falsehood, he speaks what is natural to him, for he is a liar [himself] and the father of lies and of all that is false.

Look at this, in 2 Corinthians 4:4 (AMPC) the Word also tells us that Satan has blinded the unbeliever's minds [that they should not discern the truth], preventing them from seeing the illuminating light of the Gospel of the glory of Christ (the Messiah), Who is the Image and Likeness of God.

The enemy loves to convince you that you have been so bad that God does not even want you!

Romans 11:1-2 (AMPC) Literally asks the question:

I ASK then: Has God totally rejected and disowned His people? Of course not! v2) No, God has not rejected and disowned His people [whose destiny] He had marked out and appointed and foreknown from the beginning.

This is Great News to a lot of folks! *He is not mad at you!*

Now we know that the Word says that we are "brand new" when we accept Christ as our Savior.

> 2 Corinthians 5:17 (AMPC) Therefore if
> any person is [ingrafted] in Christ (the
> Messiah) he is a new creation (a new crea-
> ture altogether); the old [previous moral
> and spiritual condition] has passed away.
> Behold, the fresh and new has come!

It is incredible to think that the "old me" is not relevant anymore! It does not matter who or what I thought I was or what I had to do or even what I did before accepting Christ as my personal Lord and Savior. It does not matter now because I have a new identity in HIM. I am His own! I have been accepted into this incredible family! I am His child!

Romans 8:15-17 (AMPC) 15. For [the Spirit which] you have now received [is] not a spirit of slavery to put you once more in bondage to fear, but you have received the Spirit of adoption [the Spirit producing sonship] in [the bliss of] which we cry, Abba (Father)! Father! 16. The Spirit Himself [thus] testifies together with our own spirit, [assuring us] that we are children of God. 17. And if we are [His] children, then we are [His] heirs also: heirs of God and fellow heirs with Christ [sharing His inheritance with Him]; only we must share His suffering if we are to share His glory.

It is easy to just read the scriptures and not understand the reality of the Word. Some people go for years and can quote scriptures, but they are never changed. Why? There is a difference in reading something and really stopping to let the message of the Word soak in and become a part of your life, a part of who you are. A lot of people read the Bible like a regular book, or a novel perhaps, but you need to stop, drop, and meditate. Stop just reading and make an effort to actu- ally let the Word become your reality. How does this work? Instead of just reading to be reading, when you come to a scripture, read a few words or a verse and then stop and really think about what this is saying, what it means, what it means for you and to you. We must come to a place where we are so solid in the *knowledge* of God's Word about us, that nothing can shake us! God's word is unshakeable and His Word in us needs to become unshakeable!

One of the questions I would ask you is this: If the world or your circle of friends or family "change your name" to whatever suits them or what they see you as or what they think they need you to be, then how does that affect your way of thinking or existing? Are you changing your language, (not literally), but the phrases or words that you would normally use, to "fit in" or be accepted, or to make yourself appear that you always have the right answer or correct response? Are you sacrificing what you really believe in to please someone else? Are you expected to act a certain way or to "go with the flow" regardless of how you really feel? I want us all to get a better understanding of *who* God says we are! He thinks you are awesome! Look at what God says:

> Jeremiah 1:5 (AMPC) Before I formed you in the womb I knew [and] approved of you [as My chosen instrument], and before you were born, I separated and set you apart, consecrating you;

> Jeremiah 31:3 (AMPC) Yes, I have loved you with an everlasting love; therefore, with loving-kindness have I drawn you and continued My faithfulness to you.

He loves you so much!!

Psalms 139:17-18 (AMPC) 17. How precious and weighty also are Your thoughts to me, O God! How vast is the sum of them! 18. If I could count them, they would be more in number than the sand.

He thinks you are the *bomb!*

CHAPTER 2

....

God's Blessings

How does knowing my identity tie into the benefits and blessings that God offers? We have listed some of the "identity" scriptures to get us to start thinking the correct way about ourselves. Knowledge is an incredible thing! Letting the Word soak in! Let the revelation of His Word become your foundation. There are benefits that are available just because of *who* you are! Blessings that are promised!

Here are just a few of the blessings and promises!

> Jeremiah 29:11 (AMPC) For I know the thoughts and plans that I have for you, says the Lord, thoughts and plans for welfare and peace and not for evil, to give you hope in your final outcome.

This scripture lets us know that that the Lord wants us to be in peace and have a good life and have a good future. He *thinks* about you!

Isaiah 41:10 (AMPC) Fear not [there is nothing to fear], for I am with you; do not look around you in terror and be dismayed, for I am your God. I will strengthen and harden you to difficulties, yes, I will help you; yes, I will hold you up and retain you with My [victorious] right hand of rightness and justice.

The phrase Fear Not or Do not be afraid is listed 365 times in the Bible! That covers every day of the year! Imagine that!

Jeremiah 17:17 (AMPC) I have a refuge and a hope!

This assures us that HE is available. A lot of people think so little of themselves and their current situation that they feel lost and hopeless.

Exodus 23:25 (AMPC) By serving the Lord God, I am blessed and healed!

Philippians 4:7 (AMPC) And God's peace [shall be yours, that tranquil state of a soul assured of its salvation through Christ, and so fearing nothing from God and being content with its earthly lot of whatever sort that is, that peace] which transcends all understanding shall garrison and mount guard over your hearts and minds in Christ Jesus.

(Notice that this states that peace *shall* be yours? Not maybe, not if…but shall!!)

Philippians 4:19 (AMPC) God supplies
ALL my needs! (all means ALL!)

Psalms 34:8 (AMPC) I trust in the Lord
and take refuge in Him and because of
this I am blessed and happy!

Then we just have to quote all of Psalms 23, AMPC version because it is just too good to pass up!

THE LORD is my Shepherd [to feed, guide, and shield me], I shall not lack. 2. He makes me lie down in [fresh, tender] green pastures; He leads me beside the still and restful waters. 3. He refreshes and restores my life (my self); He leads me in the paths of righteousness [uprightness and right standing with Him—not for my earning it, but] for His name's sake. 4. Yes, though I walk through the [deep, sunless] valley of the shadow of death, I will fear or dread no evil, for You are with me; Your rod [to protect] and Your staff [to guide], they comfort me. 5. You prepare a table before me in the presence of my enemies. You anoint my head with oil; my [brimming] cup runs over. 6. Surely or only goodness, mercy, and unfailing love shall follow me all the days of my life, and through the length of my days the house of the Lord [and His presence] shall be my dwelling place.

Good stuff! You know a lot of people know Psalms 23; they can quote it without even thinking about it. Many of us memorized it in Sunday School when we were just children, but sometimes we quote it or read it without really stopping to recognize all the great promises that it contains.

The Lord, our Shepherd leads us, guides us, feeds us, shields us. Verse one alone is enough to make you shout! But there is more! HE provides rest for us, refreshing and restoration, He is with us in the valley, we do not have to fear or dread, He is our comforter. His goodness, mercy, and love are unfailing and is *always* with us!

In Galatians 5:22-23 (AMPC) these scriptures assure us that because of His Spirit in us, we have love, joy, gladness, peace, patience, an even temper, forbearance, kindness, goodness, benevolence, faithfulness, gentleness, meekness, humility self-control, self-restraint, continence.

This is *huge*! You mean to say that "I" have these things "deposited" inside of me? The answer is *yes*!

Wait... There is more...

A summary of Matthew 5:8-9, assures me that I am Blessed, happy, fortunate, and spiritually prosperous—possessing God's favor and His grace, I am pure in heart, I have joy in my life and satisfaction, I make and maintain peace, I am a child of God! The Bible is full of the reality of who you are and what this really means!

According to 2 Corinthians 1:20, God's Promises are Yes and Amen!

> Isaiah 40:29 (AMPC) He gives power to the faint and weary, and to him who has no might He increases strength [causing it to multiply and making it to abound].

God is your strength!!

> Isaiah 40:31 (AMPC) But those who wait for the Lord [who expect, look for, and hope in Him] shall change and renew

their strength and power; they shall lift
their wings and mount up [close to God]
as eagles [mount up to the sun]; they shall
run and not be weary, they shall walk and
not faint or become tired.

What is it that we really expect in life? What do we
look for? What do we hope in? It is easy to feel weary and
sometimes feel defeated, like we have no more strength to get
through the day, but the promises listed in these scriptures
show us how God will lift us up. This promises us that even
though, at times, we feel like we cannot go on or we do not
know how we can get through a certain situation, if we look
to the Lord and put our hope in Him, He will always come
through! We have such an incredible Savior!

Psalms 68:19 (AMPC) tells us that *He
loads us daily with benefits*!

Lamentations 3:22-23 (AMPC) tells us
that His mercies are new every morning!
He is faithful!

Every day we have a brand-new opportunity to have
a fresh start with a fresh dose of His mercy and love! If you
messed up yesterday, there is good news, today is a brand-
new day! Imagine today starting out with knowing that God
is for you and not against you. What a revelation! Especially
to those who have always looked at God as a Big Ole' Dude
"up there" with a baseball bat, ready to whack you upside the
head if you do anything wrong!

Look at this verse:

> Isaiah 43:2 (AMPC) When you pass through the waters, I will be with you, and through the rivers, they will not over-whelm you. When you walk through the fire, you will not be burned or scorched, nor will the flame kindle upon you.

This scripture is a reminder of the story in Daniel 3 where three Hebrew teenagers were thrown into the fiery furnace by King Nebuchadnezzar for not bowing down to a Golden Idol that he had erected to be worshipped. He ordered Shadrach, Meshach, and Abednego to be executed for refusing to worship anything or anyone other than God Himself. The King ordered the furnace to be turned up seven times hotter than usual, and the boys to be bound and thrown into the fire. It was so hot that the guards that threw them in did not even survive the sparks from the fire. Later, when King Nebuchadnezzar looked inside the furnace, he not only saw the boys walking around, but he saw Jesus in there with them! When he ordered the boys to come out, their clothes were intact, and they did not even smell like smoke! Incredible!

This story is just a reminder that no matter what is happening in your life or what has already happened, God is always with you, He will never leave you or forsake you!

There have been times in my own life that I felt like I was not going to make it out of a situation, when hope seemed so far out of my reach. A lot of times in life we are faced with what seems like an impossible situation, where no matter which way you turn, you think that it would lead to agony or despair. But our knowing, just like Shadrach,

Meshach, and Abednego, that God is really for us and not against us, that He is the only answer, the only way, that no matter what life throws at us, we will stand up for God and boldly proclaim that He is *all* that we will ever need.

I imagine that it was such a difficult time for these guys, in reading the book of Daniel, we know that Shadrach, Meshach, and Abednego were not even their real names. When they got taken into captivity, their names were changed, they had to learn a new language, their eating habits were challenged, the culture was totally different, their God was not accepted as the true God, so therefore, their faith was challenged, hence the fiery furnace. Chapter One in the Book of Daniel states that Shadrach's real name was Hananiah, Meshach was really Mishael, and Abednego was really Azariah. One thing though, that never changed was their trust and belief in God. That foundation was the "glue" that held them together. They were not shaken in the hard times. That is so incredible to imagine!

I think a lot of times in life, people or situations try to label us or re-name us. Sometimes we may find ourselves "bowing down" to a certain idea or a certain way of living, that although, we may not be one hundred percent on board, we find ourselves bending or swaying enough to conform, enough to be accepted or to fit in as one of the crowd. Not feeling strong enough to stand up boldly and protest.

I was totally that person for a long time, so I understand! I lost several friends the day that I decided that I was no longer going to be the sober driver after a night out dancing at the club. This was a hard pill for my friends to swallow because they did not see anything wrong with my going to the club and dancing all night, and then driving all my drunk friends' home, first stopping at the liquor store and going inside to purchase booze for them.

I, thankfully, never acquired a taste for alcohol, but I loved to go dancing. The problem was that nobody would have guessed that I was "trying to be a Christian." I would be out all-night Saturday and then force myself up on Sunday morning to go to church. This has to sound familiar to someone, right? Pushing past my exhaustion and painting on my church face, I needed to present the perfect image, you know. Wow. I am shaking my head, as I write this. I would never have admitted this to my parents even though I was thirty years old. What a mess! I just trotted right in the church house like I was the sweetest little thing ever!

I know that this may not even register to some as a bad thing, but for me, if I felt like I needed to lie about where I had been, it was wrong. Needless to say, some of my friends, once they realized I was of no use to them, dropped out of my life, one by one. Why? They saw that I was not going to "compromise" anymore. I could not go on pretending to be one thing and the next day another. I was on a roller coaster ride and desperately needed to get off. I did not want to be that person anymore that was always willing to compromise because it just led to a guilty conscience and a lot of depressing days.

> Deuteronomy 31:6 and verse 8, (AMPC)
> 6. Be strong, courageous, and firm; fear not nor be in terror before them, for it is the Lord your God Who goes with you; He will not fail you or forsake you. 8. It is the Lord Who goes before you; He will [march] with you; He will not fail you or let you go or forsake you; [let there be no cowardice or flinching, but] fear not, neither become broken [in spirit—

depressed, dismayed, and unnerved with alarm].

This next scripture we find in Hebrews brings it out in a great way, three times God says that He will not leave you!

> Hebrews 13:5(b), (AMPC) He (God) Himself has said, I will not in any way fail you nor give you up nor leave you without support. [I will] not, I will] not, [I will] not in any degree leave you helpless nor forsake nor let [you] down (relax My hold on you)! [Assuredly not!]

Wow, what a Promise!

> Isaiah 54:10 (AMPC) Gods love and kindness shall not depart from you, nor shall the covenant of peace and completeness be removed,

> Isaiah 54:17 (AMPC) no weapon that is formed against you shall prosper, and every tongue that rises against you in judgment will be shown to be in the wrong. This [peace, righteousness, security, triumph over opposition] is the heritage of the servants of the Lord.

This next one is huge, this tells us that if we *believe*, He promises to answer prayers!

Mark 11:24 (AMPC) whatever you ask for in prayer, believe (trust and be confident) that it is granted to you, and you will [get it].

You mean that God actually hears my prayers and *will* indeed answer? Yes!

Matthew 21:22 (AMPC) And whatever you ask for in prayer, having faith and [really] believing, you will receive. The question here for you is, what are you really believing? Are you really believing that God will come through or is it laced with doubt? Some people believe that God will do a thing for someone else but maybe not for them. This is where we need to remember that God shows no partiality and is no respecter of persons.

Romans 2:11 (AMPC) For God shows no partiality [undue favor or unfairness; with Him one man is not different from another].

Acts 10:34 (AMPC) And Peter opened his mouth and said: Most certainly and thoroughly I now perceive and understand that God shows no partiality and is no respecter of persons.

The enemy would have you believe that because of "who you are" or what you have done, that you are not worthy enough to have your prayers answered. Sometimes, it may not the devil at all, but you, convincing yourself that God does not really care enough to answer. This one goes back to identity in Christ and the reality of who you are because of Him. I believe that our feelings of unworthiness are due to a lack of understanding what the blood of Jesus actually did for us! He shed His blood and died on the cross for our salvation. When He forgives someone of all their sins, He means *all* of the sins, not just some of them. When He said that He would cast our sin in the "sea of forgetfulness," He meant it.

> Micah 7:19 (AMPC) He will again have compassion on us; He will subdue and tread underfoot our iniquities. You will cast all our sins into the depths of the sea.

The problem is, is that we like to go deep sea fishing, and reel it all back in! We also tend to forget that He cast our sin out as far as the east is from the west!

> Psalms 103:12 (AMPC) As far as the east is from the west, so far has He removed our transgressions from us.

We tend to forget this sometimes though. Why do we forget, how could we possibly forget? People reminding us of the past for one, but also just a guilty conscience, and sometimes of course, the enemy likes to remind us and make us question if we are really even saved. In Proverbs 3:5-6, the scriptures tell us that we can Lean on Him, we can trust Him, we can be confident in Him. We need to stop trying to rely on our own insight and understanding. Most things are beyond our natural understanding. We need to come to know God, to recognize Him, to acknowledge Him because He will direct our steps. If we let Him.

That is sometimes the problem though, we want to try to figure everything out on our own. It is hard, at times to "let go and let God."

Why do you think that is? I think that society today teaches us to have ability within ourselves, to think for ourselves, to be self-sufficient, create and achieve our own goals. The thought that is missing in this though, is that without God, we cannot do anything.

Without God, we cannot have lasting peace or self-worth. If we do not have a solid foundation of *who* God is and *who* we are *because* of Him, we simply cannot get very far in life because inevitably, we will get caught up in our "lack" of identity. We will always be looking for something better, something bigger, more ways to "make" a thing happen, and frankly, when it becomes all about me, me, me, the more unhappy and distraught we can become. There seems to always be something that says we need more, we want more, and then how can we make it happen? It can turn into a pretty miserable cycle.

> Romans 10:11-12 (AMPC) The Scripture says, 'No man who believes in Him [who adheres to, relies on, and trusts in Him] will [ever] be put to shame or be disappointed. 12. [No one] for there is no distinction between Jew and Greek. The same Lord is Lord over all [of us] and He generously bestows His riches upon all who call upon Him [in faith].'

Acts 17:28 (AMPC) For in Him we live
and move and have our being; For we are
also His offspring.

So, the question is "Who are you calling on?"

Are you calling on yourself to get "life" done, or are you calling on the One who *is* life? The same one who gave you life?

He holds all of your answers.

CHAPTER 3

....

Who Is God?

We have been talking about God and how wonderful He is, but there are a lot of ideas about Him and His character that are incorrect. Earlier, I referred to some folks picturing Him as a big old dude with a baseball bat ready to beat on them for doing wrong. Unfortunately, this really is how some people think. Some people live in fear of Him, they feel like they can never measure up to His expectations and because of this they feel separated from Him or abandoned by Him because of past mistakes. These ideas can lead to feelings of isolation, humiliation, depression, anxiety, or guilt.

Do you really think that this is what God wants for us? Of course not! In the Bible, there are a lot of descriptions of Him and His characteristics, but not all of them are what God Himself actually said about Himself, some are what man said about Him. I want us to look at some of the ways that God characterizes Himself.

GOD IS LOVE (per 1 John 4:8, KJV)

> 1 John 4:9-10 (KJV) tells us that God
> (in His Love) sent His only begotten Son

so that we might live through Him. Not because we loved Him but because He loved us! Wow!

1 John 3:1 (AMPC) SEE WHAT [an incredible] quality of love the Father has given (shown, bestowed on) us, that we should [be permitted to] be named and called and counted the children of God! And so, we are!

Here is a scripture that we are all familiar with: John 3:16 (KJV) For God so loved the world, that He gave His only begotten Son, that whosoever believeth in Him should not perish but have everlasting life.

John 3:17 (KJV) For God sent not His Son into the world to condemn the world; but that the world through Him might be saved.

Imagine such a love that God has for us!

1 John 4:10 (AMPC) In this is love: not that we loved God, but that He loved us and sent His Son to be the propitiation (the atoning sacrifice) for our sins.

Possibly the most "famous" love scriptures are found in 1 Corinthians 13, depicting how love should be portrayed. Most messages taught about love will usually contain these passages. It is usually preached that we should endeavor to obtain this way of living, showing, and expressing love to others, which is a correct assumption, but let us look at it in a different manner; If God *is* Love, it sheds a new light on the revelation of this. Watch what happens by replacing the word "love" with the name "God."

> 1 Corinthians 13:4-8(a) Adapted from (AMPC) 4. God endures long, God is patient, and God is kind; God never is envious, God never boils over with jealousy, God is not boastful or vainglorious, God does not display Himself haughtily. 5. God is not conceited, God is not arrogant, God is not inflated with pride; God is not rude, God is not unmannerly, God does not act unbecomingly. God does not insist on His own rights or His own way, for God is not self-seeking; God is not touchy, God is not fretful, God is not resentful; God takes no account of the evil done to Him and God pays no attention to a suffered wrong]. 6. God does not rejoice at injustice and unrighteousness; God rejoices when right and truth prevail. 7. God bears up under anything and everything that comes, God is ever ready to believe the best of every person, God's hopes are fadeless under all circumstances, and God endures everything [without weakening]. 8. God never fails [never fades out or becomes obsolete or comes to an end].

Can you say, "wow?" Anything other than these characteristics about God is wrong. If you think anything contrary to this, you have been mistaken about *who* God really is. He Loves you! He wants to have a relationship with you. He sent His own Son, Jesus, so that He can have a relationship with us. Look at this next scripture:

> Isaiah 43:25 (AMPC) I, even I, am He Who blots out and cancels your transgressions, for My own sake, and I will not remember your sins.

"What? This is Huge! This is God actually saying that He forgives us not for *our* sake, but because *He* wants a relationship with us! Jesus died for our salvation, Yes, He bore the stripes on His back for our healing, Yes, we are going to heaven and not hell, Praise God! But these are all in addition to The Father God wanting relationship. This is a game changer!"

> Zephaniah 3:17 (AMPC) The Lord your God is in the midst of you, a Mighty one, a Savior [Who saves]! He will rejoice over you with joy; He will rest [in silent satisfaction] and in His love He will be silent and make no mention [of past sins, or even recall them]; He will exult over you with singing.

This is one of my favorite verses in Scripture! When I discovered this verse, I almost fell out of my chair! Imagine that He is excited to see you, to spend time with you, He is satisfied with you, and *He* is singing a song over *you*! I like to picture God dancing with glee and singing a little love song to me! Can you imagine? A personalized song, Yes, you and I, my dear friend, are loved!

This is an incredible revelation because I have met a lot of people along the way that have very little faith that God actually even cares about them. The reasons for this can vary from trauma to drama. A lot of people feel trapped in a life situation that is far from perfect, maybe dealing with guilt, confusion, depression, or illness. Whatever the situation may be, they can have a wrong perception about God and His actual nature. Let us look at a story in the book of Mark.

> Mark 1:40-42 (AMPC) 40. And a leper came to Him, begging Him on his knees and saying to Him, 'If You are willing, You are able to make me clean.' 41. And being moved with pity and sympathy, Jesus reached out His hand and touched him, and said to him, I am willing; be made clean! 42. And at once the leprosy [completely] left him and he was made clean [by being healed].

Now keeping in mind, the Scripture where Jesus said If you have seen Me, You have seen the Father. (Ref: John 14:9 AMPC) it also states this earlier in the same book, (John 1:18 AMPC) No man has ever seen God at any time; the only unique Son, or the only begotten God, Who is in the bosom [in the intimate presence] of the Father, He has declared Him [He has revealed Him and brought Him out where He can be seen; He has interpreted Him and He has made Him known].

This account of the leper in Mark, talks about Jesus being moved with pity and sympathy and when asked "Will you heal me?" Jesus replied without hesitation, "Of course, I am willing!" He, being full of love for this man, wanted to heal him. Imagine that kind of love! Even though the man was "unclean" due to the leprosy, Jesus reached out and touched him! This is the kind of thing that any Father would do for their own child, if they could!

The man's question was not, "Can you heal me, but will you?"

I think that this is a relevant question on people's minds today. *Yeah but, will He?*

Jesus has the same response today that He had then "Of course I want to, and I will!" What would a good and perfect parent want for you? The very best! For you to be healed and restored. This is why Jesus went about doing good, performing miracles, healing the sick, etc. To be that example of what God "our" Father wanted to portray, to show Himself to be caring, loving, compassionate. Not just to His Son Jesus, but to you and me, His sons and daughters! Remember the prayer that Jesus prayed that starts with *Our Father* (Luke 11:2) not just His Father, but *our* Father also! God loves us *all*, the same, He does not have a favorite kid! He makes the statement again in John chapter 17.

> John 17:21-23 (AMPC) 21. That they all may be one, [just] as You, Father, are in Me and I in You, that they also may be one in Us, so that the world may believe and be convinced that You have sent Me. 22. I have given to them the glory and honor which You have given Me, that they may be one [even] as We are one:

23. I in them and You in Me, in order that they may become one and perfectly united, that the world may know and [definitely] recognize that You sent Me and that You have loved them [even] as You have loved Me.

This is incredible! Jesus is saying that God loves us the same way that He loves Him! This is mind blowing! And it goes on to say what I mentioned earlier that Jesus was the accurate portrayal of God! Jesus is perfect theology, the perfect example of *who* the Father is!

John 17:24-26 (AMPC) 24. Father, I desire that they also whom You have entrusted to Me [as Your gift to Me] may be with Me where I am, so that they may see My glory, which You have given Me [Your love gift to Me]; for You loved Me before the foundation of the world. 25. O just and righteous Father, although the world has not known You and has failed to recognize You and has never acknowledged You, I have known You [continually]; and these men understand and know that You have sent Me. 26. I have made Your Name known to them and revealed Your character and Your very Self, and I will continue to make [You] known, that the love which You have bestowed upon Me may be in them [felt in their hearts] and that I [Myself] may be in them.

We see His character being revealed the more that we dig into the Word. When we see the story of Jesus healing the sick, the blind, the deaf, raising the dead…the stories are endless.

> John 21:25 (AMPC) And there are also many other things which Jesus did. If they should be all recorded one by one [in detail], I suppose that even the world itself could not contain (have room for) the books that would be written.

But with each story, we see that God is Love!

> Luke 11:11-13 (AMPC) 11. What father among you, if his son asks for a loaf of bread, will give him a stone; or if he asks for a fish, will instead of a fish give him a serpent? 12. Or if he asks for an egg, will give him a scorpion? 13. If you then, evil as you are, know how to give good gifts [gifts that are to their advantage] to your children, how much more will your heavenly Father give the Holy Spirit to those who ask and continue to ask Him!

He wants to load us down with blessings and grace and gifts!

> John 1:16 (AMPC) For out of His fullness (abundance) we have all received [all had a share, and we were all supplied with] one grace after another and spiri-

tual blessing upon spiritual blessing and even favor upon favor and gift [heaped] upon gift.

1 Corinthians 1:9 (AMPC) God is faithful (reliable, trustworthy, and therefore ever true to His promise, and He can be depended on); by Him you were called into companionship and participation with His Son, Jesus Christ our Lord.

Growing up and in living my life, I wish that I had understood this. I always felt like there was something missing. I struggled with loneliness and depression, and I could not really figure out why. I was not taught about a personal relationship with Jesus. Even though I was raised in church, the sermons were usually about reaching the lost and getting people saved, which is great, we all need to be a witness for Jesus, but I did not realize that there was more...or how to even achieve more.

Once you get saved, then what? That was my struggle. What now? I honestly spent a lot of my time thinking that God was mad at me, that I was a huge disappointment to Him because of wrong choices and wrong attitudes. I would do something wrong and then lose sleep because I thought I was going to hell for my mistake that day, I found myself repenting and repenting again and worrying and then repenting some more, apologizing multiple times for being such a disappointment. I learned a whole lot about guilt and had so much fear that I would not make it into heaven, I was a wreck! I had more questions than answers. I felt like I had multiple personalities at times, I was acting one way at church, one way at home, one way at work, one way with my "Christian friends" and another way with my non-Christian friends. I did not even know who I was, other than a depressed mess in a dress. Does any of this sound familiar?

It took really getting into God's Word and digging deeper into *Him* before I finally started seeing a difference. Did it happen overnight? If only. I wasted a lot of years trying to be something that God never called me to be.

How about you? My advice is to seek God! More and more and more! He is the Answer. Renew your mind about who you thought God was and what kind of unrealistic expectations you may have had about yourself. God loves you just the way you are, you were not a surprise to Him! He created you in such a perfect and loving way, you could never be such a disappointment that He would change His mind about loving you! He is the ultimate Father! Full of love for you!

> Isa 41:10 (AMPC) Fear not [there is nothing to fear], for I am with you; do not look around you in terror and be dismayed, for I am your God. I will strengthen and harden you to difficulties, yes, I will help you; yes, I will hold you up and retain you with My [victorious] right hand of rightness and justice.

HE is our helper, He is our strengthener, He is always available to hold us and to comfort us!

> Isa 51:12 (AMPC) I, even I, am He Who comforts you.

He is all we need! I encourage you to study Him, get to know Him, to strive to have a better understanding of who He is. It is so easy to get caught up in situations of life and feel like you are not worthy to have an incredible relationship with Him, but He is not judging you on what you do for Him or not do for Him, He loves you just because *you* are His favorite kid!

CHAPTER 4

....

Pressing into God

Psalms 16:8-11 (AMPC) 8. I have set the
Lord continually before me; because He
is at my right hand, I shall not be moved.
9.Therefore my heart is glad and my glory
[my inner self] rejoices; my body too
shall rest and confidently dwell in safety,
10(a). For You will not abandon me 11.
You will show me the path of life; in Your
presence is fullness of joy, at Your right
hand there are pleasures forevermore.

This is really packed with promise! Imagine living in a state
of not being moved, knowing that I will not be abandoned,
that I can live feeling safe and full of gladness! What a concept! To some, this may seem like an impossibility, they could
not even imagine living a life that even remotely sounds like
this. I run into a lot of people in life that if you were to ask
them a simple question like "What do you want out of life?"
almost everyone would state that they just want to be happy.

This sounds simple enough, doesn't it? Just that one request, happiness. The only question that remains is how?

People everywhere are on a quest, a pursuit of happiness. Oh, to just have a little joy, a little peace, to be able to rest, to clear the clutter. Well, we can see what the Word says back up in verse 11 of Psalms 16, it starts with "I have set the Lord continually before me." Okay, Stop. This is key... Start with a question to self: "Have I set the Lord before me?" Let us examine ourselves for just a moment. Where do you see growth in your life? Are you growing in your career, reputation, achievements, relationships with friends or loved ones, social skills? Do you see that you are growing more in these areas than you are growing in grace and revelation? Have you found that you are so enveloped in achieving and or maintaining a level of success that you have forgotten to stop and press into God and all that He has prepared for you? It is easy to get caught up in the hustle and bustle of everyday life and put God on the back burner. It is not really that we intend for this to happen, it just does. Maybe we simply don't know how to really put Him first.

That was my problem for many years, and honestly it is a process, a re-training of self, an everyday purposeful attempt to seek God first before anything else. There is an old hymnal that just simply says:

> "In the morning when I rise,
> In the morning when I rise,
> In the morning when I rise, Give me Jesus.
> Give me Jesus, Give me Jesus,
> You may have all this world
> Give me Jesus."

This should be our truth, that simple thought "Just give me Jesus." How that single phrase alone can become a huge part of who we are, how we get through life, how we approach our day. Just give me Jesus. There is a difference in how we look at our circumstances when we look for Jesus first, seeking Him at all times, in every situation, every day. It is not a difficult search, as some may think, pressing into Him, is as simple as speaking His Name. *Jesus.* He is always just one breath away. He is always that close!

> Deuteronomy 30:14 (AMPC) But the word is very near you, in your mouth and in your mind and in your heart, so that you can do it.

Remembering that Jesus *is* the Word, and He longs for you and longs for a relationship with you, He longs to spend time with you, He longs to show you just who He is. He is seeking you just as much, or actually more, than you seek Him.

> 2 Chronicles 16:9 (AMPC) For the eyes of the Lord run to and fro throughout the whole earth to show Himself strong on behalf of those whose hearts are blameless toward Him.

> John 4:23 (AMPC) A time will come, however, indeed it is already here, when the true (genuine) worshipers will worship the Father in spirit and in truth (reality); for the Father is seeking just such people as these as His worshipers.

Once we get into His presence, there is the answer!

> Psalms 16:11 (AMPC)... In Your pres-
> ence is fullness of joy.

> Jeremiah 29:11-14 (AMPC) 11. For I
> know the thoughts and plans that I have
> for you, says the Lord, thoughts and
> plans for welfare and peace and not for
> evil, to give you hope in your final out-
> come. 12. Then you will call upon Me,
> and you will come and pray to Me, and I
> will hear and heed you. 13. Then you will
> seek Me, inquire for, and require Me [as
> a vital necessity] and find Me when you
> search for Me with all your heart. 14. I
> will be found by you, says the Lord, and
> I will release you from captivity.

We are using these scriptures often out of Jeremiah, but for good cause, they are full of great news that we need to be reminded of again and again. This gives us some insight on the benefits of calling on the Lord and seeking His face. It assures us that not only does He hear us, He listens, and also answers, and He promises that He will indeed be found and will indeed release us from whatever has been holding us back. We all have our own definition of what is holding us "captive." It could be stress, anxiety, family drama, work issues, financial issues, health issues, we have all had our own issues in life, but thank God, He is available to help us, to redeem our lives from the pit!

Ps 103:3-6 (AMPC) 3.Who forgives [every one of] all your iniquities? Who heals [each one of] all your diseases? 4. Who redeems your life from the pit and corruption? Who beautifies, dignifies, and crowns you with loving-kindness and tender mercy? 5. Who satisfies your mouth [your necessity and desire at your personal age and situation] with good so that your youth, renewed, is like the eagle's [strong, overcoming, soaring]? 6. The Lord executes righteousness and justice [not for me only, but] for all who are oppressed.

We need to make a decision to "turn" and this is not necessarily talking about repentance, although repentance is certainly one the most important aspects in life, I am not negating Salvation at all, just emphasizing the importance of looking and seeking and pressing into Him.

1 Chronicles 16:8-11 (AMPC) 8. O give thanks to the Lord, call on His name; make known His doings among the peoples! 9. Sing to Him, sing praises to Him; meditate on and talk of all His wondrous works and devoutly praise them! 10. Glory in His holy name; let the hearts of those rejoice who seek the Lord! 11. Seek the Lord and His strength; yearn for and seek His face and to be in His presence continually!

2 Chronicles 7:14 (AMPC) If My people, who are called by My name, shall humble themselves, pray, seek, crave, and require of necessity My face and turn ..., then will I hear from heaven, forgive their sin, and heal their land.

I know a lot of people today are looking for answers, looking for healing in many areas, not just in their health, there are so many "layers" to us sometimes that we do not even know how to approach life or the challenges of the day. We have questions that no one seems to know the answers to, we have dilemmas that may be blocking our path to peace. Here is what the Lord says:

Jeremiah 33:2-3 (AMPC) 2. Thus says the Lord Who made [the earth], the Lord Who formed it to establish it—the Lord is His name: 3. Call to Me and I will answer you and show you great and mighty things, fenced in and hidden, which you do not know (do not distinguish and recognize, have knowledge of and understand).

Luke 11:9-10 (AMPC) 9. So I say to you, 'Ask and keep on asking and it shall be given you; seek and keep on seeking and you shall find; knock and keep on knocking and the door shall be opened to you. 10. For everyone who asks and keeps on asking receives; and he who seeks and keeps on seeking finds; and to him who

knocks and keeps on knocking, the door
shall be opened.'

It is *all* in *Him*! Who knew, right? This is incredible
news, but we still might have a but... You may still be saying "But how does this really work, how can I do this and
get results?" My personal answer is *Worship*. Now we have
talked a little bit about how God is seeking true worship.
Remember this verse from earlier...

John 4:23 (AMPC) A time will come,
however, indeed it is already here, when
the true (genuine) worshipers will worship the Father in spirit and in truth
(reality); for the Father is seeking just
such people as these as His worshipers.

What exactly is Worship? Great question!
Here is what the Merriam-Webster Dictionary says
about the word worship:

1. To honor or show reverence for as a divine being or
   supernatural power.
2. To regard with great or extravagant respect, honor
   or devotion. This word is being used here as a verb,
   meaning there is action behind it. A few Synonyms
   for the word worship are: adore, glorify, revere.

So how are we to worship? When we shift all our attention onto Jesus, when we get into a mode of heartfelt adoration and an awe of who He is and what He means to us,
realizing how absolutely Holy and Wonderful He is. We love
to praise, which to me, is different in the sense that praise can

be loud at times, boisterous, joyful, clapping, lifting hands to Him, which is incredible! I love to give Him Praise, He is so worthy of it, but worship, true worship, is a more intimate way of being in His presence. Worship should be for Him alone!

> Luke 4:8 (AMPC)…You shall do homage to and worship the Lord your God, and Him only shall you serve.

Now taking a look at the word Praise, the definition by the Merriam-Webster dictionary is this:

1. To express a favorable judgment of
2. To glorify (a god or a saint) especially by the attribution of affections.

Again, using this word as a verb, synonyms of the word praise are: Bless, celebrate, exalt, extol, glorify, magnify These thoughts certainly are to be used in Praise.

> Ps 75:1 (AMPC) WE GIVE praise and thanks to You, O God, we praise and give thanks; Your wondrous works declare that Your Name is near and they who invoke Your Name rehearse Your wonders. Praise to God is what we offer in acknowledging His excellence!

It is not the same as a thank you, but it certainly is similar in that we are thanking Him for all that He is and all that He has done, but we cannot stop at just a simple "thanks" when we are Praising Him. Thanksgiving describes our attitude toward what He has done, while Praise is offered for who He is in our lives. He is indeed worthy of our Praise!

> Psalms 18:3 (KJV) I will call upon the LORD, who is worthy to be praised as believers we should realize that we were created to Praise Him!

> Isaiah 43:21 (AMPC) The people I formed for Myself, that they may set forth My praise [and they shall do it].

> Hebrews 13:15 (AMPC) Through Him, therefore, let us constantly and at all times offer up to God a sacrifice of praise, which is the fruit of lips that thankfully acknowledge and confess and glorify His name.

Praise originates in a heart that is full of love for Him!

> Deuteronomy 6:5 (AMPC) And you shall love the Lord your God with all your [mind and] heart and with your entire being and with all your might.

Praise can be expressed in different ways; we are probably most familiar with expressing it in song or in prayer. The book of Psalms tells us to praise at all times.

> Psalms 34:1-3 (AMPC)1. I WILL bless the Lord at all times; His praise shall continually be in my mouth. 2. My life

> makes its boast in the Lord; let the hum-
> ble and afflicted hear and be glad. 3. O
> magnify the Lord with me and let us
> exalt His name together.

Can you imagine if His praise was continually in your mouth? What kind of difference would we actually see in our lives if this was the case? There are so many things to praise God for! The things that He has done, the situations that He has brought us through, for His holiness, His mercy, His kindness and goodness, His grace, Salvation! This is a continual list! It is hard to stand still when we actually think on and consider who He is in our lives and where would we be without Him. It is exciting news when we consider all of these things! No wonder we are loud and boisterous!

He is Worthy! The Bible tells us that when He comes again that all mankind will acknowledge Him as Lord!

> Philippians 2:9-11 (AMPC) 9. Therefore
> [because He stooped so low] God has
> highly exalted Him and has freely
> bestowed on Him the name that is above
> every name, 10. That in (at) the name
> of Jesus every knee should (must) bow,
> in heaven and on earth and under the
> earth, 11. And every tongue [frankly and
> openly] confess and acknowledge that
> Jesus Christ is Lord, to the glory of God
> the Father.

> Psalms 113:1-3 (AMPC) 1. PRAISE
> THE Lord! (Hallelujah!) Praise, O ser-
> vants of the Lord, praise the name of the

Lord! 2. Blessed be the name of the Lord
from this time forth and forever 3. From
the rising of the sun to the going down of
it and from east to west, the name of the
Lord is to be praised!

So now we can discuss Worship a little bit more…
Worship is about losing self in the adoration of Him. Praise
is an entryway to worship, but it goes beyond the gates of
praise. Worship gets to the heart of who we are by the will-
ingness to humble ourselves, to surrender everything to Him,
to adore Him not for what He has done or what He can do
for you, but just simply because of Who He is. Worship is a
lifestyle!

Psalms 95:6 (AMPC) O come, let us
worship and bow down, let us kneel
before the Lord our Maker [in reverent
praise and supplication].

Psalms 99:5 (AMPC) Extol the Lord our
God and worship at His footstool! Holy
is He!

Revelation 4:11 (AMPC) Worthy are
You, our Lord and God, to receive the
glory and the honor and dominion, for
You created all things; by Your will they
were [brought into being] and were
created.

Through worship we can realign our priorities with His,
acknowledging Him as Lord of our lives. Worship is indeed a

form of surrender. It is impossible to worship God and anything else at the same time, it is all or nothing. We need to gain an attitude of worship where we can quiet our spirit and mind and just focus solely and entirely on His majesty, His Glory, His awesomeness, it is an attitude of the heart.

God sees the heart, regardless of what other people may see you do. On the outside just lifting your hands with the rest of the crowd in a service perhaps, may not mean very much, but when God sees the real you, seeking Him, seeking His presence, losing yourself in the magnitude of *Him*, when He sees your heart and realizes that you are lost in the moment, that nothing else matters, this is His desire.

He deserves sincere, heartfelt worship! In that reality, you will know that He is truly worthy, truly amazing, and nothing else matters in that moment, Just Him! Having an encounter with Him and being in a state of mind where nothing else exists in that moment but the magnitude of Him! To totally surrender everything, every thought, every fear, every doubt, every worry, getting caught up in the splendor of His excellence, where nothing matters but this encounter, your focus is solely on the Creator of the Universe and His glory. No words could even begin to describe His Holiness! It is enough to leave you completely wrecked on the floor in a puddle of tears! No words are needed in this moment! Just Him!

> James 4:8 (KJV) Draw nigh to God, and
> He will draw nigh to you.

Yet another great promise! We cry out for more of you Lord, more of you! Less of me, more of you! This is our desire for the more of *You* Lord!

When we realize that the only thing that matters is You, Oh Lord, all the worries of the day just melt away in your presence! What an incredible thing! All of us need more of God, and so we continually seek His face.

For in His Presence there if fullness of joy!

CHAPTER 5

....

Encountering Jesus

In our journey to grow and learn more about Jesus and what this relationship means to us and how it can affect every area and aspect of our lives, we may find ourselves seeking more answers about how to "get" more of Him. We may hear stories and testimonies of Jesus doing miraculous things for people or how that meeting Him has totally changed their lives, how they were lost and pitiful before, but now, they are brand new and life is better, and they have peace and joy finally.

This all sounds incredible, for them, right? But what about me and what about you? What do I need to do to get this "new" incredible life? What is it about Jesus that make people change, or want to change? We can look back at His disciples, when He chose them there was no hesitation on their part, they just followed Him.

> Luke 5:11(b) (AMPC) they left every-
> thing and joined Him as His disciples
> and sided with His party and accompa-
> nied Him.

Matthew 4:19-20 (AMPC) 19 And He said to them, 'Come after Me [as disciples—letting Me be your Guide], follow Me, and I will make you fishers of men!' 20 At once they left their nets and became His disciples [sided with His party and followed Him].

Imagine dropping everything and running after Jesus. This is exactly what happened. There was something incredible about Jesus, apparently! At once, they ran after Him! What are you running after? Great question. What am I running after? We really need to stop and examine ourselves and see what we find. What is the desire of your heart? You hear a lot of people say the words, "Oh, yes, I want to be in His presence, I want to do what He says, I want to feel Him, I want to be in peace, oh yes, I do need Him!"

But when they stop to really examine their hearts, there seems to be a hindrance. Something that is keeping them from really seeking and really staying on the right path.

Mouthing a bunch of words does not necessarily mean a heart change. A lot of people say a lot of things, but what is in the heart? Looking at the disciples, they were just a bunch of ordinary guys doing ordinary things, most of them were simple fishermen, they had jobs, businesses, families. The different stories we read in the Bible talk about them, perhaps in the middle of their work day, encountering Jesus, not really knowing anything about Him, but they dropped everything, because there was *something* about Jesus, something that was different, so different from anything or anyone that they had encountered before, something extraordinary that made them suddenly change their minds about what they were doing and in that moment, doing a complete 180 and leaving all of their previous thoughts and activities behind to follow Jesus! And with just running in the direction of Jesus, these ordinary people, set out on a course that would change all of history!

What a mindset these guys had! It is hard to imagine, really imagine, dropping everything to follow Jesus! I think that people today need to encounter Jesus, I mean really encounter Him.

They are pleading for a life change, something…to make a difference, maybe folks that have been in church for a long time that are still just muddling through, just trying to make it, climbing up the rough side of the mountain, getting knocked down and stomped on, beat up, feeling worthless and defeated, not knowing how to get out of their depressive state of being. They may be feeling like they don't even have enough energy to even try sometimes. They need an encounter, but not just an encounter, a life changing encounter!

Let's look at the Apostle Paul's Story…

> Acts 9:1-6 (AMPC) 9:1. MEANWHILE SAUL, still drawing his breath hard from threatening and murderous desire against the disciples of the Lord, went to the high priest 2. And requested of him letters to the synagogues at Damascus [authorizing him], so that if he found any men or women belonging to the Way [of life as determined by faith in Jesus Christ], he might bring them bound [with chains] to Jerusalem. 3. Now as he traveled on, he came near to Damascus, and suddenly a light from heaven flashed around him, 4. And he fell to the ground. Then he heard

a voice saying to him, Saul, Saul, why are you persecuting Me [harassing, troubling, and molesting Me]? 5. And Saul said, Who are You, Lord? And He said, I am Jesus, whom you are persecuting. It is dangerous and it will turn out badly for you to keep kicking against the goad [to offer vain and perilous resistance]. 6. Trembling and astonished he asked, Lord, what do You desire me to do? The Lord said to him, but arise and go into the city, and you will be told what you must do.

Okay, some back story, Paul (Saul), same guy, Saul was his Jewish name and Paul was actually his Roman name; We see him starting to use Paul in Acts 13:9. He was originally an enemy of Christians, his goal was to lock them all up and, in some cases, see that they were executed. He was a Jew and not a believer that Jesus was actually the Son of God, the Messiah.

He was what we may call a "big-wig" in the government of his day, he studied under a famous rabbi of that time named Gamaliel and he mastered Jewish history, the Psalms and the work of the prophets. He learned Jewish law to the point of becoming a lawyer and all signs pointed to him becoming a member of the Sanhedrin, the Jewish Supreme Court. He was zealous for his faith and did not allow for any compromise. It was this same zeal that led him down a road of becoming a religious extremist, some say a religious terrorist. He became determined to eradicate Christians, ruthless in his pursuit, because he actually believed that he was acting in the name of God. In Acts 8:3, it states that, "he shamefully treated and laid waste the church continuously [with cruelty and violence]; and entering house after house, he dragged out men and women and committed them to prison."

He was living a life full of anger and rage against the Christians. This is where we see the scene played out on his way to Damascus back up in Acts 9. This meeting with Jesus along the way, completely changed his life! It tells us that he was totally preoccupied with his task, convinced that he was doing the right thing, the "only thing" that he knew to do, he certainly never expected to be falling off his "high horse" as it were, in the blinding presence of Jesus Christ Himself!

Can you imagine such a thing? All he could do in that moment was become a trembling mess on the ground! From that moment on, his life was turned upside down! The encounter that literally changed his whole being!

How many of us today are just going about, living life, doing what we do, maybe not even realizing that we are pursuing the wrong things or not even realizing that there is something more? I say that we need an encounter, not just any old encounter, but a life changing, soul changing, mind changing encounter with *Him*, that will knock us off our horses and into the incredible presence of Jesus Christ, the Son of the Living God!

A lot of folks may feel like that they can never really have this kind of experience, maybe because of their past. First, we learn that Jesus saves, forgives, heals, and delivers, regardless of what you have done. The remarkable story of Paul repeats itself daily, as people all over the world are transformed by God's saving grace in Jesus. Some of these people have done horrible things, while others are just trying to live a "moral" life thinking, *Oh, I am a good person and maybe that will be enough.*

We see that in the story of Paul, how people in his day could not fathom that God would "save" him after all that he had done, he was a murderous thug! But the beauty of salvation, is that God saves *all* mankind, regardless of what "kind of man" you were before! You may not "feel" worthy to receive forgiveness but thank the Lord that it is *not* based on our feelings of worthiness or unworthiness. It is based on His love for us! Hallelujah!

The truth is that everyone matters to God, from the "good, decent, average" person, to the "wicked, evil, degenerate" one. Only God can save a soul from hell. Little known fact about "sin" is that there is no little, big, bigger, or biggest sin, in the eyes of God. Sin is sin. Man has labeled sin as little or worse, but God has not!

> James 2:10 (AMPC) For whosoever keeps the Law [as a] whole but stumbles and offends in one [single instance] has become guilty of [breaking] all of it.

> Matthew 12:31(a) (AMPC) Therefore I tell you; every sin and blasphemy (every evil, abusive, injurious speaking, or indignity against sacred things) can be forgiven men.

This is great news! God forgives everything, anything, regardless of how you, others or society looks upon it. This is shouting news! I know a lot of people that are convinced that they have done such horrendous deeds that there is no hope, no absolute forgiveness. But the news is in: Headline: The Blood of Jesus was enough!

This is where you should be doing your Happy Dance!

Okay, now that we have that settled, let's go back to "Encountering Jesus." The first question again is "how?" One answer is "seek His face."

> Psalms 105:2-5(a) (AMPC) 2. Sing to Him, sing praises to Him; meditate on and talk of all His marvelous deeds and devoutly praise them. 3. Glory in His holy name; let the hearts of those rejoice who seek and require the Lord [as their indispensable necessity]. 4. Seek, inquire of and for the Lord, and crave Him and His strength (His might and inflexibility to temptation); seek and require His face and His presence [continually] evermore. 5. [Earnestly] remember the marvelous deeds that He has done, His miracles and wonders.

> Psalms 27:8 (AMPC) You have said, 'Seek My face [inquire for and require My presence as your vital need]. My heart says to You, Your face (Your presence), Lord, will I seek, inquire for, and require [of necessity and on the authority of Your Word].

> Psalms 27:13-14 (AMPC) 13. [What, what would have become of me] had I not believed that I would see the Lord's goodness in the land of the living! 14. Wait and hope for and expect the Lord; be brave and of good courage and let your

heart be stout and enduring. Yes, wait for and hope for and expect the Lord.

Isaiah 58:9(a) (AMPC) Then you shall call, and the Lord will answer; you shall cry, and He will say, Here I am.

When we call, He will answer when we seek Him, we will find Him!

What are you seeking? What are you hoping for, what are you waiting for, what are you expecting?

If your first response is not Jesus, then you need to change your response. Only an encounter with Him can change your life, completely, totally, one hundred percent! To change and never be the same, that is one of the greatest quests in life.

CHAPTER 6

....

Renewing Your Mind

Romans 12:2 (AMPC) Do not be conformed to this world (this age), [fashioned after and adapted to its external, superficial customs], but be transformed (changed) by the [entire] renewal of your mind [by its new ideals and its new attitude], so that you may prove [for yourselves] what is the good and acceptable and perfect will of God, even the thing which is good and acceptable and perfect [in His sight for you].

Ephesians 4:22-24 (AMPC) 22. Strip yourselves of your former nature [put off and discard your old unrenewed self] which characterized your previous manner of life and becomes corrupt through lusts and desires that spring from delusion; 23. And be constantly renewed in the spirit of your mind [having a fresh mental and spiritual attitude], 24. And put on the new nature (the regenerate self) created in God's image, [Godlike] in true righteousness and holiness.

Okay, so, how in the world do we "renew" our minds? Great question. For me, I had to realize that my thinking was all wrong. I thought that I had to be like everyone else, I had to fit in. I had wrong ideas about my identity (in Christ), wrong ideas about how my life was going to be, how I was going to survive this situation or that circumstance, I was a mess! The enemy "the thought thrower" was having a field day with my mind! I was never going to be good enough or have enough or just be enough, period. I know people like that today, that have the same problem. They get caught up in their own thoughts about a thing and try to rationalize a situation without thinking about what God has to say about it.

Isaiah 55:8-9 (AMPC) 8. For My thoughts are not your thoughts, neither are your ways My ways, says the Lord. 9. For as the heavens are higher than the earth, so are My ways higher than your ways and My thoughts than your thoughts.

First, identity in Christ is the thing that can most influence your situation, and that also helps to determine your future. This happens by faith. What is faith? Faith is not hope, faith is knowledge, it is a knowing. Our faith has to be rooted in Christ and what He says, otherwise it is not really faith.

Hebrews 11:1 (AMPC) NOW FAITH is the assurance (the confirmation, the title deed) of the things [we] hope for, being the proof of things [we] do not see and the conviction of their reality [faith perceiving as real fact what is not revealed to the senses].

This scripture is saying that faith is real fact and proof of things we do not see. It is not just a wish. This sheds a new light on what we may have previously thought about the definition.

In order to understand "the battle" that is going on inside of us, we must understand that the flesh likes to be in control, it has always been in control. From the day that we were born, we have been ruled by our flesh. When you accept Jesus into your life, then Holy Spirit moves in, and urges you to do things contrary to what your flesh prefers. An easy example is your flesh would rather be lazy and not read the Word of God, it would rather watch television instead, but what would Jesus want you to do? Seek His Word, of course.

How do we "get" faith?

Romans 10:17 (KJV) So then faith cometh by hearing and hearing by the word of God.

Faith comes. When, how? By hearing the Word. Knowledge of what God says about us and our lives is the key factor.

Galatians 5:16-17 (AMPC) 16. But I say, walk and live [habitually] in the [Holy]

71

Spirit [responsive to and controlled and guided by the Spirit]; then you will certainly not gratify the cravings and desires of the flesh (of human nature without God). 17. For the desires of the flesh are opposed to the [Holy] Spirit, and the [desires of the] Spirit are opposed to the flesh (godless human nature); for these are antagonistic to each other [continually withstanding and in conflict with each other], so that you are not free but are prevented from doing what you desire to do.

Sounds like a war is going on between our flesh and spirit. The Apostle Paul talks about this in depth in the book of Romans. Let's start with Chapter 7 and verse 14:

Romans 7:14-25 (AMPC) 14. We know that the Law is spiritual; but I am a creature of the flesh [carnal, unspiritual], having been sold into slavery under [the control of] sin.

Verse 15 says He it is baffled at the things that he does sometimes, Yikes!

15. For I do not understand my own actions [I am baffled, bewildered]. I do not practice or accomplish what I wish, but I do the very thing that I loathe [which my moral instinct condemns]. 16. Now if I do [habitually] what is con-

trary to my desire, [that means that] I acknowledge and agree that the Law is good (morally excellent) and that I take sides with it.

17. However, it is no longer I who do the deed, but the sin [principle] which is at home in me and has possession of me.

Verse 17 can get a little confusing if you don't understand that the new you, the new Spirit that is deposited in you, is Perfect, because that "part" is actually the Holy Spirit from God Himself, (how could God have any imperfections?) He can't.

18. For I know that nothing good dwells within me, that is, in my flesh. I can will what is right, but I cannot perform it. [I have the intention and urge to do what is right, but no power to carry it out.] 19. For I fail to practice the good deeds I desire to do, but the evil deeds that I do not to do are what I am [ever] doing.

Do you feel like all you ever do, is make terrible choices and bad decisions? You may try to do what is pleasing to the Lord, and you want to do what is pleasing, but sometimes you just fall short.

20. Now if I do what I do not desire to do, it is no longer I doing it [it is not myself that acts], but the sin [principle] which dwells within me [fixed and operating

in my soul]. 21. So I find it to be a law (rule of action of my being) that when I want to do what is right and good, evil is ever present with me and I am subject to its insistent demands. 22. For I endorse and delight in the Law of God in my inmost self [with my new nature]. 23. But I discern in my bodily members [in the sensitive appetites and wills of the flesh] a different law (rule of action) at war against the law of my mind (my reason) and making me a prisoner to the law of sin that dwells in my bodily organs [in the sensitive appetites and wills of the flesh]. 24. O unhappy and pitiable and wretched man that I am! Who will release and deliver me from [the shackles of] this body of death?

This is *huge*. We may think that we just cannot be free, we may feel unhappy, pitiable, and wretched. *But God!*

25. O thank God! [He will!] through Jesus Christ (the Anointed one) our Lord! So then indeed I, of myself with the mind and heart, serve the Law of God, but with the flesh the law of sin.

New Attitude!

We need a new attitude, a new way of looking at life, at looking at ourselves. No more "going with the flow" of the crowd. How can I "renew" my thinking if I am continually filling myself with negativity? How can I possibly change if I continually do the same things that I always did? Am I taking time out of my day to pray, to read and meditate on His Word? You can't really expect to change if you only go to church for one hour on Sunday. The enemy doesn't mind if you go to church, it is only when you start to learn and apply the Word to your life that he will get agitated. There is a difference in going somewhere and *going* somewhere. Does your journey consist of multiple pit stops or are you determined to go and keep going until you arrive at your destination?

I was raised in church, being the daughter of a Pastor, we were always at church or some sort of church function. There was never a question of "are we going to church today?" We knew that we were going, no doubts at all, it was our "duty." So, you would think that I knew the Bible, that I was "on it" and loving every minute of it, that I was learning, studying, applying the Word to my life, but you would be wrong. First, I was only going because I had to, second, I was going to sing because I loved to sing and play piano, third, I had friends that went to my church. So, where was my relationship with God? Was it strong, was it growing, was I growing? It was just a "Sunday" kind of relationship. Was I maturing in Christ? No. Was I really paying attention to the preacher? Not really, I was too busy being a social butterfly and gossiping with my friends. Does any of this sound familiar? Did I know that I needed more of God? I would say, sort of yeah, but I was always willing to compromise, willing to wait until a more opportune time or do what I wanted to for a while and then repent for it later. My frame of thinking was kind of like the story in Exodus when the Pharaoh was asked to let God's people go, after a series of plagues hit Egypt, Pharaoh opted to keep the frogs "one more day."

Exodus 8:1-10 (AMPC) 1. THEN THE Lord said to Moses, Go to Pharaoh and say to him, Thus says the Lord, Let My people go, that they may serve Me. 2. And if you refuse to let them go, behold, I will smite your entire land with frogs; 3. And the river shall swarm with frogs which shall go up and come into your house, into your bedchamber and on your bed, and into the houses of your servants and upon your people, and into your ovens, your kneading bowls, and your dough. 4. And the frogs shall come up on you and on your people and all your servants. 5. And the Lord said to Moses, 'Say to Aaron, 'Stretch out your hand with your rod over the rivers, the streams and canals, and over the pools, and cause frogs to come up on the land of Egypt." 6. So, Aaron stretched out his hand over the waters of Egypt, and the frogs came up and covered the land. 7. But the magicians did the same thing with their enchantments and secret arts and brought up [more] frogs upon the land of Egypt. 8. Then Pharaoh called for Moses and Aaron, and said, 'Entreat the Lord, that He may take away the frogs from me and my people; and I will let the people go that they may sacrifice to the Lord.' 9. Moses said to Pharaoh, 'Glory over me in this: dictate when I shall pray [to the Lord] for you, your servants, and your people, that the frogs may be destroyed from you and your houses and remain only in the river.' 10. And [Pharaoh] said, 'Tomorrow.' [Moses] said, 'Let it be as you say, that you may know that there is no one like the Lord our God.'

In reading this story, you would think, why in the world would the Pharaoh want to sleep with the frogs one more night? Yet how many of us are doing the same thing, thinking, *Oh, just one more day…let me do what I want to, and I will "repent" tomorrow*, or in my own personal case, next Sunday. How many of us just opt to "keep the frogs" just a little while longer? I am sure enjoying myself, I don't want to think about the consequences of my actions tonight, I know what God wants and wants for me, *but…*

This is a prime example of the war between the spirit and the flesh. The flesh wants to keep the frogs, it does not want to compromise at all. What are your frogs? Drug addiction, alcohol addiction, hatred, envy, jealousy, pride, bitterness, unforgiveness, addiction to gaming (this one is huge), social media addiction, abusive behavior, harmful relationships? Feel free to add your own "frog" to this list. What is your destination? Where is it? How do you achieve this goal? All good questions.

Romans 12:2 (AMPC) Do not be conformed to this world (this age), [fashioned after and adapted to its external, superficial customs], but be transformed (changed) by the [entire] renewal of your mind [by its new ideals and its new atti-

tude], so that you may prove [for your-
selves] what is the good and acceptable
and perfect will of God, even the thing
which is good and acceptable and perfect
[in His sight for you].

For me, the most difficult part of changing was to realize
that I was not created to sin. That was *not* what God had in
mind when He created man. He created man to be like Him,
in His very image, and to have a relationship with Him. He
wanted to be able to have someone that would willingly want
to spend time with Him and want to be close to Him, someone with a free will to *choose* a relationship with Him.

I was always trying to fit in, trying to be just like everyone else, trying to be popular or likeable, looking for love in
all the wrong places. I was on a quest to "find myself" and in
the process I would compromise on my beliefs, compromise
on how to find happiness and peace, compromising myself
so that I would be liked.

As I searched for a solution to my misery, I found myself
depressed, feeling defeated, worthless, not good enough,
angry, stressed, I did not like myself at all. I tell this and
people often wonder how, if I was raised in church, how I
could be struggling with anything, how things were not just
falling into place in my life. The answer is the inner battle.
I did not know anything about identity in Christ, I did not
know that there was power in my words, I did not have any
faith, I had plenty of doubt instead. I did not know enough
of the Word of God to use it as a tool or a weapon, I was
stuck in a cycle of defeat and did not realize that I needed a
new way of living life, or if I knew that I did need it, I did not
know how to go about getting it. I did not know that I could
find freedom. So, going back to the original thought that just

going to church, will not change you. It took me a long, long time to realize that I needed more of the Word and I could never get to where I needed to be or wanted to be without that knowledge.

> John 8:32 (KJV) And ye shall know the truth, and the truth shall make you free.

So now, let's look at Ephesians.

> Ephesians 4:22-24 (AMPC) 22. Strip yourselves of your former nature [put off and discard your old unrenewed self] which characterized your previous manner of life and becomes corrupt through lusts and desires that spring from delusion; 23. And be constantly renewed in the spirit of your mind [having a fresh mental and spiritual attitude], 24. And put on the new nature (the regenerate self) created in God's image, [Godlike] in true righteousness and holiness.

This is telling us that we have been born again, and we have a new "man" that is deposited in us, called Holy Spirit. Our old man, or our old "self" still wants to be in control, it has been in control since the day we were born, and it has no intention of giving up this seat of power without a fight. You may not have noticed it much before because our thought has always been, "Oh, this is just how I am" or, the best one is, "this is how I was raised" Or, "this is my daily routine, how I live my life." Our goal is to crucify the old man, our old self, and be raised up in the new nature and image of God.

How do we do this? One word quickly comes to my mind: Starvation. You have to weaken that sucker!

> Romans 13:14 (AMPC) But clothe yourself with the Lord Jesus Christ (the Messiah) and make no provision for [indulging] the flesh [put a stop to thinking about the evil cravings of your physical nature] to [gratify its] desires (lusts). Let's define the word Provision: (per Merriam-Webster-Dictionary)

* The act or process of providing. (noun)
* To supply with needed materials. (verb)

In our lives we have always been taught to be controlled by the five senses: touch, taste, see, smell, hear. Anything that is outside of these factors is what most folks label "unnatural," hence, the spiritual aspect is automatically rejected when it tries to override the "natural" way we have always existed in life. The problem is, when we let it control our flesh, it can potentially affect our stand on faith and our spirit. We know that the flesh is our mind, will and emotions, so when starting our new journey with Jesus, it is more than easy to just "be" the way we always were, because anything contrary to that takes discipline. Is there any hope to overcome? Yes! But like anything else, it will not happen overnight, it is a matter of growth. So, let's look at how to weaken the flesh by way of "starvation."

Like anything, if you cut off the supply or provision for a thing, it will get weak. For instance, if you have a house plant, it will flourish if it has ample light and water, but if you neglect to water it and or if you put it in a dark room, it will start to wither and eventually it will die. Our flesh and spirit are warring against each other, but which one will come out "on top" is going to be based on how we feed it, what we feed it, and how often we feed it. Is it subject to the light or to the darkness? If you starve your flesh by feeding your spirit, then obviously the spirit will become stronger and begin to "overpower" the flesh. This is the power of "fasting." You are literally starving the flesh while feeding the spirit with the Word and with prayer, humility and obedience to God and His commandments. Your flesh is learning the word "no." You must apply this principle to every area of the flesh such as immorality, idolatry, distractions, emotions, even the types of entertainment you are seeking.

What are you watching, what are you listening to? In every area of fleshly desire that you find yourself struggling with, you must decide to have a good old fashioned "fasting" mentality. If the flesh is strong and the spirit is weak, then you need to declare a fast of the thing that the flesh desires, this is what will start forcing the flesh into submission. In order to deprive it of power you have to train the flesh to start yielding its will and what it wants, to the spirit. It is a constant and also a conscious effort to force it to obey when it doesn't want to. When you deny your flesh what it wants by giving your spirit what it needs, you feed and strengthen the spirit while starving and weakening the flesh, until finally, the desires of the flesh start to die, and you are finally able to be controlled by the spirit. We all want our "spirit man" to be strong. God's plan for us is that we be all we can be through Him.

Holy Spirit is given to us to lead us, guide us, comfort us, encourage us, and to be a constant cheerleader for our growth in the ways of Christ. He (Holy Spirit) is there to teach us how to be over comers. Honestly, I had never really given much thought to Holy Spirit and what He is or even Who He is. I thought that the Holy Spirit was something that came upon me when I was really feeling God, you know those Holy Ghost do-dads or Holy Ghost chill bumps, once I was finished shouting or jumping or raising my hands, once I "calmed down" it "just left," I seriously had no idea that Holy Spirit was a *He* and that *He* was always, always on the inside of me once I received Jesus as my personal Lord and Savior. I told you, even though I grew up in church, I was pretty clueless. Sad.

> Romans 8:13-15 (AMPC) 13. For if you live according to [the dictates of] the flesh, you will surely die. But if through the power of the [Holy] Spirit you are [habitually] putting to death (making extinct, deadening) the [evil] deeds prompted by the body, you shall [really and genuinely] live forever. 14. For all who are led by the Spirit of God are sons of God. 15 For [the Spirit which] you have now received [is] not a spirit of slavery to put you once more in bondage to fear, but you have received the Spirit of adoption [the Spirit producing sonship] in [the bliss of] which we cry, Abba (Father)! Father

> 1 Corinthians 3:1-3 (AMPC) 1. HOWEVER, BRETHREN, I could not talk to you as to spiritual [men], but as to nonspiritual [men of the flesh, in whom the carnal nature predominates], as to

mere infants [in the new life] in Christ [unable to talk yet!] 2. I fed you with milk, not solid food, for you were not yet strong enough [to be ready for it]; but even yet you are not strong enough [to be ready for it], 3. For you are still [unspiritual, having the nature] of the flesh [under the control of ordinary impulses]. For as long as [there are] envying and jealousy and wrangling and factions among you, are you not unspiritual and of the flesh, behaving yourselves after a human standard and like mere (unchanged) men?

How would someone define you? What is more dominate in your life? Would they say that you are "totally" sold out to your flesh or would they recognize that you are strong in spirit? The longer that you yield to the spirit, the easier it will become to ignore the appetites of the flesh. I, for one, don't want to remain unchanged. Let's look at the book of Galatians.

Galatians 5:16-25 (AMPC) 16. But I say, walk and live [habitually] in the [Holy] Spirit [responsive to and controlled and guided by the Spirit]; then you will certainly not gratify the cravings and desires of the flesh (of human nature without God). 17. For the desires of the flesh are opposed to the [Holy] Spirit, and the [desires of the] Spirit are opposed to the flesh (godless human nature); for these are antagonistic to each other [contin-

ually withstanding and in conflict with
each other], so that you are not free but
are prevented from doing what you desire
to do. 18. But if you are guided (led) by
the [Holy] Spirit, you are not subject to
the Law. 19. Now the doings (practices)
of the flesh are clear (obvious): they are
immorality, impurity, indecency, 20.
Idolatry, sorcery, enmity, strife, jealousy,
anger (ill temper), selfishness, divisions
(dissensions), party spirit (factions, sects
with peculiar opinions, heresies), 21.
Envy, drunkenness, carousing, and the
like. I warn you beforehand, just as I did
previously, that those who do such things
shall not inherit the kingdom of God.

This is a pretty intense list! I am sure we could think of
some other things that we have dealt with in our own lives
that the Apostle Paul did not mention. Maybe there are some
things in your life that would make some folks cringe to even
think about. The struggle is real! Let's read some more:

22. But the fruit of the [Holy] Spirit
[the work which His presence within
accomplishes] is love, joy (gladness),
peace, patience (an even temper, forbearance), kindness, goodness (benevolence),
faithfulness, 23. Gentleness (meekness,
humility), self-control (self-restraint,
continence). Against such things there is
no law [that can bring a charge]. 24. And
those who belong to Christ Jesus (the

Messiah) have crucified the flesh (the godless human nature) with its passions and appetites and desires.

There is hope! This lets us know that because of Holy Spirit living inside of us, we actually have joy, peace, patience, etc. We don't have to wish and pray and plead and long for these things, it's all part of the package!

25. If we live by the [Holy] Spirit, let us also walk by the Spirit. [If by the Holy Spirit we have our life in God, let us go forward walking in line, our conduct controlled by the Spirit.]

We need to recognize that He, Holy Spirit, that dwells inside of the Christian, is the promise that Jesus made that *we* will never be alone! If we need help or guidance or strength, Holy Spirit provides all these things.

John 14:16-17 (AMPC) 16. And I will ask the Father, and He will give you another Comforter (Counselor, Helper, Intercessor, Advocate, Strengthener, and Standby), that He may remain with you forever—17. The Spirit of Truth, Whom the world cannot receive (welcome, take to its heart), because it does not see Him or know and recognize Him. But you know and recognize Him, for He lives with you [constantly] and will be in you.

2 Corinthians 5:17 (AMPC) Therefore if any person is [ingrafted] in Christ (the Messiah) he is a new creation (a new creature altogether); the old [previous moral and spiritual condition] has passed away. Behold, the fresh and new has come!

John 1:12-13 (AMPC) 12. But to as many as did receive and welcome Him, He gave the authority (power, privilege, right) to become the children of God, that is, to those who believe in (adhere to, trust in, and rely on) His name—13. Who owe their birth neither to bloods nor to the will of the flesh [that of physical impulse] nor to the will of man [that of a natural father], but to God. [They are born of God!]

I don't want you to read all of this and think, *War, Fight, Battle*, this is a lot to take in, I understand that. You may be thinking about the old adage, "I am a lover and not a fighter." Jesus wants us to be aware that there is help and there is hope. Some stay in such dire straits, not even realizing that Holy Spirit is available, they have no clue that He is gentle and loving and beautiful and caring and wants us to live the best life possible! Remember that He came so that you may have and enjoy life and have it in abundance! (ref: John 10:10)

Imagine actually enjoying life! Some think that it is impossible, but He is the God that makes all things possible!

CHAPTER 7

....

What is the Holy Spirit?

So, we have been talking a little bit about Holy Spirit. But some people, like I used to be, have no idea what Holy Spirit is or what He does. Taking a deeper, closer look at the role of Holy Spirit lets us come to a better understanding of the Trinity, God the Father, God the Son, God the Holy Spirit.

> Genesis 1:26-27 (AMPC) 26. God said, 'Let Us [Father, Son, and Holy Spirit] make mankind in Our image, after Our likeness, and let them have complete authority over the fish of the sea, the birds of the air, the [tame] beasts, and over all of the earth, and over everything that creeps upon the earth.' 27. So God created man in His own image, in the image and likeness of God He created him; male and female He created them.

These scriptures tell us that God created us in His image and in His likeness. This is a topic that can be a little confusing because here it states that He made us a two-part being, image first, likeness second. We look like Him in image, and we have a mind, will and emotions, like Him also. However, it does not say here that we receive the Holy Spirit. Yet. This happens after we get saved.

Look at what Jesus says regarding the Holy Spirit:

> John 14:16-17 (AMPC) 16. And I will ask the Father, and He will give you another Comforter (Counselor, Helper, Intercessor, Advocate, Strengthener, and Standby), that He may remain with you forever—17. The Spirit of Truth, Whom the world cannot receive (welcome, take to its heart), because it does not see Him or know and recognize Him. But you know and recognize Him, for He lives with you [constantly] and will be in you.

> John 16:7 (KJV) Nevertheless I tell you the truth; It is expedient for you that I go away: for if I go not away, the Comforter will not come unto you; but if I depart, I will send Him unto you.

According to these scriptures, Jesus makes us believe that the Holy Spirit was not inside of man before His death and resurrection. The Holy Spirit would come upon someone or alongside someone for strength, power, etc. according to the Bible, we see this a lot in the Old Testament and also some in the New Testament. You may ask what is the difference in upon or inside? This seems clear cut actually, inside a person, literally means inside. You are probably familiar with the old saying "I accepted Jesus into my heart and He now lives on the inside of me," This is literally what it means. When the spirit comes upon a person to help do a thing, it will eventually leave, but once He actually comes inside, He is there to stay, forever!

Take a look at this conversation between Jesus and His disciples, after Jesus had resurrected:

> Acts 1:5 and 8 (AMPC) 5. For John baptized with water, but not many days from now you shall be baptized with (placed in, introduced into) the Holy Spirit. 8. But you shall receive power (ability, efficiency, and might) when the Holy Spirit has come upon you, and you shall be My witnesses in Jerusalem and all Judea and Samaria and to the ends (the very bounds) of the earth.

This is an account of what happened at Pentecost, several weeks after the above conversation:

> Acts 2:1-4(a) (AMPC) 1. AND WHEN the day of Pentecost had fully come, they were all assembled together in one place, 2. When suddenly there came a sound from heaven like the rushing of a violent tempest blast, and it filled the whole house in which they were sitting. 3. And there appeared to them tongues resembling fire, which were separated and distributed, and which settled on each one of them. 4. And they were all

filled (diffused throughout their souls)
with the Holy Spirit ...

I admit that I had spent most of my Christian life thinking that Holy Spirit or Holy Ghost was just an experience, I referred to it earlier as Holy Ghost do-dads, or chill bumps, a lot of jumping, running, etc., hearing folks speak in tongues, it was a big time until it just left, the "feeling" just left. No one at my home church had ever told me or taught me anything differently. I just assumed that what I saw others doing, or what I was feeling was the only thing that Holy Spirit did. I had always heard about The Father, Son, and the Holy Spirit, but I never really made a distinctive separation in my mind about it. So, now that I have a better understanding that I am *now*, after accepting Jesus Christ as my personal Lord and Savior, a three part being. Flesh, Soul, and *now* Spirit.

I guess a good question that I should have been asking a long time ago is "What exactly changes in my life once I accept Jesus Christ?" If I had already been made in the image and likeness of God and at that point, I automatically had the Holy Spirit inside of me at the time of my creation, then what would have been the point in Jesus dying for the sins of the world? To make a way for us to go to Heaven and not hell, yes, Amen for that. But is that all there would have been? (Don't misunderstand, I am NOT insinuating that that is NOT enough) This question goes back to how would I be able to make it through any situation or circumstance if there wasn't something more? If I did not have a helper or strengthener, or a source of peace, how could I possibly survive? How could anyone? So, I want to try to break this down a bit more.

Once we repent and accept Jesus into our lives, at that point Holy Spirit is deposited inside of us. It is a brand-new life now! The "old man" is now dead, and the "new man" shows up on the scene! You have now received Holy Spirit. He will never leave you, never. He is inside now to help you, to lead you, to guide you. He has so many different jobs!

In the book of John, Chapters 14-16 (AMPC) there are at least 32 things listed about Holy Spirit.

1. Comforter
2. Counselor
3. Helper
4. Intercessor
5. Advocate
6. Strengthener
7. Standby
8. Remain with you Forever
9. The Spirit of Truth
10. HE lives with you constantly
11. He will be in you
12. Teach you all things
13. He will cause you to recall (will remind you of, bring to your remembrance) everything I have told you.
14. Who comes (proceeds from the Father)
15. Testify regarding Me. (Jesus)
16. I will send Him to you (to be in close fellowship with you).
17. Convict and convince the world
18. About sin.
19. About righteousness (uprightness of heart and right standing with God)
20. About judgment

21. Truth-giving Spirit
22. He will Guide you into all the Truth (the whole, full truth)
23. He will speak His own message (on His own authority)
24. He will tell whatever He hears (from the Father, He will give the message that has been given to Him)
25. He will announce and declare to you the things that are to come (that will happen in the future)
26. Honor Jesus
27. Glorify Jesus
28. He will take of (receive, draw upon) what is Jesus'
29. He will reveal
30. He will declare
31. He will disclose
32. He will transmit to you.

Can we say "wow?" And this is not all of what Holy Spirit is for! This is just a little bit! If you take a look at the role/roles of Holy Spirit, it is incredible to think that *all* of Him and *all* that He offers, is available! He will always point you in the right direction, which of course, always leads you back to Jesus and His perfect will for your life. Holy Spirit is sometimes referred to as a gift, but clearly, we can see that He is so much more than a gift. Realizing that He is ready and willing to help you, teach you, comfort you, etc. is an incredible thing! So, if we start understanding more about Him, we can see how He will be able to grow and become stronger the more we draw from Him, the more we study God's Word, the more we seek God, the more we seek His face, His presence, this is a sure-fire way to give Holy Spirit more reign in your life. In learning more about Holy Spirit, we can start getting a clearer picture now of how the flesh wars against the Spirit. The flesh always wants its own way, but if we lean on and depend on Holy Spirit more and more, He will teach us how to be over comers, how to live a victorious life, how to have peace in the midst of a storm, the good news in all of this is that He wants you to understand that you *already* have *all* of these wonderful attributes inside of you because He is inside of you now! We just need to step it up a few notches and live like a winner! Remember that you are blessed and highly favored! Hallelujah!

> Ephesians 3:16-21 (AMPC) 16. May He grant you out of the rich treasury of His glory to be strengthened and reinforced with mighty power in the inner man by the [Holy] Spirit [Himself indwelling your innermost being and personality]. 17. May Christ through your faith [actually] dwell (settle down, abide, make His permanent home) in your hearts! May you be rooted deep in love and founded securely on love, 18. That you may have the power and be strong to apprehend and grasp with all the saints [God's devoted people, the experience of that love] what is the breadth and length and height and depth [of it]; 19. [That you may really come] to know [practically, through experience for yourselves] the love of Christ, which far surpasses mere knowledge [without experience]; that you may be filled [through all your being] unto all the fullness of God [may have the richest measure of the divine Presence, and

become a body wholly filled and flooded with God Himself]! 20. Now to Him Who, by (in consequence of) the [action of His] power that is at work within us, is able to [carry out His purpose and] do superabundantly, far over and above all that we [dare] ask or think [infinitely beyond our highest prayers, desires, thoughts, hopes, or dreams]—21. To Him be glory in the church and in Christ Jesus throughout all generations forever and ever. Amen (so be it).

Learning to hear Holy Spirit is a lifelong task, you don't just arrive at it. You will always be learning more and more by reading the Word and developing your ability by His Word with Holy Spirit to help discern truth from error. We can never diminish the written Word of God, Holy Spirit will only be reminding, giving instruction and inspiration all based on the Word. Don't get discouraged!

Galatians 6:9 (MSG) So let's not allow ourselves to get fatigued doing good. At the right time we will harvest a good crop if we don't give up or quit.

With the help of Holy Spirit, He will show you that you already are an overcomer! You will start walking and talking and displaying confidence in your journey with the Lord! I am so excited for you! Once you realize that you actually possess everything you need, your life will radically change!

So, get acquainted with Him and start this radical new journey through life!

CHAPTER 8

....

The Power of Words

Proverbs 18:21 (AMPC) Death and life
are in the power of the tongue, and they
who indulge in it shall eat the fruit of it
[for death or life].

A lot of us know this scripture by heart. We have read it,
heard it, even quoted it, but do we understand it? Question
of the day. I think that we may have a tendency to just quote
something and then go on with our day like it did not really
matter. Does it really make a difference in my life? We say a
lot of things, but most of the time, we have no idea what we
are doing when we speak.

Have you ever noticed that you may be having a great
day, be in a great mood, the sun is shining, and all of the sud-
den someone walks in with a bad attitude and a rotten mood
and the whole atmosphere changes? Interesting how that can
happen. What kind of words were spoken? What kind of attitude was apparent? It can almost be a tangible moment and

can have the potential to ruin a perfectly good day, in just a matter of minutes. This can be powerful stuff!

The reality of the impact of just a few choice words. Some people probably grew up in a household that taught "If you don't have anything good to say, then don't say anything at all." This is great advice although, a lot of times we don't remember the lesson. It is so easy to get caught up in our feelings or a situation that is taking place and just start letting our tongue have control.

Let's take a look at a few scriptures that talk about this.

> James 3:7-10 (AMPC) 7. For every kind of beast and bird, of reptile and sea animal, can be tamed and has been tamed by human genius (nature). 8. But the human tongue can be tamed by no man. It is a restless (undisciplined, irreconcilable) evil, full of deadly poison. 9. With it we bless the Lord and Father, and with it we curse men who were made in God's likeness! 10. Out of the same mouth come forth blessing and cursing. These things, my brethren, ought not to be so.

This is a little rough. In verse 8 the tongue is referred to as being restless, undisciplined, evil, full of poison! I have encountered people in my lifetime that have totally fit this description, haven't you? Wow!

> Ephesians 4:29-32 (AMPC) 29. Let no foul or polluting language, nor evil word nor unwholesome or worthless talk [ever] come out of your mouth, but only such

[speech] as is good and beneficial to the spiritual progress of others, as is fitting to the need and the occasion, that it may be a blessing and give grace (God's favor) to those who hear it. 30. And do not grieve the Holy Spirit of God [do not offend or vex or sadden Him], by Whom you were sealed (marked, branded as God's own, secured) for the day of redemption (of final deliverance through Christ from evil and the consequences of sin). 31. Let all bitterness and indignation and wrath (passion, rage, bad temper) and resentment (anger, animosity) and quarreling (brawling, clamor, contention) and slander (evil-speaking, abusive or blasphemous language) be banished from you, with all malice (spite, ill will, or baseness of any kind). 32. And become useful and helpful and kind to one another, tenderhearted (compassionate, understanding, loving-hearted), forgiving one another [readily and freely], as God in Christ forgave you.

This covers a long list doesn't it? The problem is that it is so easy to get into the habit of speaking whatever hits your brain. When you get a bad report from the doctor or from your boss, or a situation has come up in your finances or in your relationship, how easy is it to just start confessing all of the negativities? All of the what ifs? Is it reaction to fear?

It makes me wonder, looking back at Adam and Eve in the beginning, when they did wrong, the first thing that happened was they started walking in fear. They were used to walking with God and having a solid relationship with Him, but when He came looking for them after they ate of the fruit, the scripture says that they were instantly afraid.

> Genesis 3:8-10(a) (AMPC) 8. And they heard the sound of the Lord God walking in the garden in the cool of the day, and Adam and his wife hid themselves from the presence of the Lord God among the trees of the garden. 9. But the Lord God called to Adam and said to him, Where are you? 10. He said, I heard the sound of You [walking] in the garden, and I was afraid

I know you may be thinking, *what the heck does fear have to do with my words?* Well, let's think about it for a moment; If you get a negative report from the doctor, the first thought that hits you may be "What could this mean? What is going to happen now, or what if this situation is irreversible?" Sound familiar? I think this does actually look like fear. That is exactly what the enemy loves.

> John 10:10 (AMPC) The thief comes only in order to steal and kill and destroy. I came that they may have and enjoy life, and have it in abundance (to the full, till it overflows).

If the enemy can steal your peace, perhaps with the use of a negative report, then he can potentially have the upper hand in the situation, he would love to destroy your hope!

I know a lot of people that absolutely talk themselves into a frenzy! Every word is filled with the worst-case scenario. When facing a situation in life sometimes people forget about the promises of God and the blessings that He has for His children.

All that the devil can do is throw thoughts at you, remember that he is the ultimate thought thrower, but it is up to you to receive the thought and keep it, stewing on it and worrying about it, or you can quickly remember that God is bigger! So much bigger than your circumstance!

> Deuteronomy 30:19 (AMPC) I call heaven and earth to witness this day against you that I have set before you life and death, the blessings and the curses; therefore, choose life, that you and your descendants may live.

What are you choosing? In remembering that life and death are in the power of the tongue, what are your words and confessions really saying?

Is this easy? I would have to say no, especially if you have never been taught this principle. I talk to a lot of folks that say, "I am in pain and I can't help but say negative things about my life right now." Okay, I get it, but this is where we must train our flesh to submit to the spirit that is inside of us now, especially in remembering that Jesus already died for our healing. He does not have to come back down to earth again and be beaten and crucified once more. The one time was enough!

A lot of people have negative thought patterns regarding many situations, not just pain related problems. I was the kind of person for most of my life that did not care at all to tell you about all my troubles and woes, I loved to complain, complain, complain, did I mention complain?

I was the kind of person that when you see them coming you duck in the other direction because you were just sick of hearing it... *Oh no not again...* Yes, that kind of person. I was so wrapped up in my bad mood that it would almost make me angry to see someone else having a good day, I wanted everyone around me to be frustrated too. How dare them be jolly and in a good mood when I was angry or upset. It did not matter that I woke up that way or got in that mood before I even saw them. They would come in laughing or smiling and I could not imagine *how* they could be this way at a "time like this" or in this particular environment.

It was so funny because when I would hear that no one wanted to be around me and no one liked me, I could not even begin to understand what the problem was. It certainly could not have been me, there had to have been some kind of misunderstanding. I was certainly not going to "own" it because I was completely blind to the truth. I can blame it on "being raised that way" and that is partially true, I suppose, but I had absolutely no knowledge of the power of my words, how they could impact my life and those around me. Clueless! I had no prior teaching about this topic and I certainly had not read enough of the Bible to have a good grasp on the teaching.

Your words have creative power! Bombshell! When you say something out loud enough times, it can literally become truth, not only in your own mind but also in the people around you that are continually hearing your confession. Begin to choose the words that you speak on purpose, making a conscious effort to do so. Practice self-awareness over the words that you are using to describe yourself or your situation. Negative words like can't, shouldn't, or won't, should really be avoided in your speech. Why? Because they can strip you of your ability to manifest the kind of life that you want to live and the kind of life that God wants you to live!

Let's look again at John 10:10 (b) (AMPC) I came that they may have and enjoy life, and have it in abundance (to the full, till it overflows).

Here are a few more scriptures regarding our words:

> Psalms 19:14 (AMPC) Let the words of my mouth and the meditation of my heart be acceptable in Your sight, O Lord, my [firm, impenetrable] Rock and my Redeemer.

> Psalms 34:13 (AMPC) Keep your tongue from evil and your lips from speaking deceit.

> Psalms 141:3 (AMPC) Set a guard, O Lord, before my mouth; keep watch at the door of my lips.

> Proverbs 10:19 (AMPC) In a multitude of words transgression is not lacking, but he who restrains his lips is prudent.

> Proverbs 10:31-32 (AMPC) 31. The mouths of the righteous (those harmonious with God) bring forth skillful and godly Wisdom, but the perverse tongue shall be cut down [like a barren and rotten tree]. 32. The lips of the [uncompromisingly] righteous know [and therefore

utter] what is acceptable, but the mouth of the wicked knows [and therefore speaks only] what is obstinately willful and contrary.

Proverbs 12:17-19 (AMPC) 17. He who breathes out truth shows forth righteousness (uprightness and right standing with God), but a false witness utters deceit. 18. There are those who speak rashly, like the piercing of a sword, but the tongue of the wise brings healing. 19 Truthful lips shall be established forever, but a lying tongue is [credited] but for a moment.

Proverbs 13:3 (AMPC) He who guards his mouth keeps his life.

Proverbs 15:1-2 (AMPC) 1. A SOFT answer turns away wrath, but grievous words stir up anger. 2. The tongue of the wise utters knowledge rightly, but the mouth of the [self-confident] fool pours out folly.

Proverbs 15:4 (AMPC) A gentle tongue [with its healing power] is a tree of life, but willful contrariness in it breaks down the spirit.

Proverbs 15:28 (AMPC) The mind of the [uncompromisingly] righteous studies how to answer, but the mouth of the wicked pours out evil things.

Proverbs 16:24 (AMPC) Pleasant words are as a honeycomb, sweet to the mind and healing to the body.

Proverbs 17:27 (AMPC) He who has knowledge spares his words, and a man of understanding has a cool spirit.

Proverbs 21:23 (AMPC) He who guards his mouth, and his tongue keeps himself from troubles.

Proverbs 25:11 (AMPC) A word fitly spoken and in due season is like apples of gold in settings of silver.

Proverbs 31:26 (AMPC) She opens her mouth in skillful and godly Wisdom, and on her tongue is the law of kindness [giving counsel and instruction].

Matthew 12:34-37 (AMPC) 34. You offspring of vipers! How can you speak good things when you are evil (wicked)? For out of the fullness (the overflow, the superabundance) of the heart the mouth speaks. 35. The good man from his inner good treasure flings forth good things, and the evil man out of his inner evil storehouse flings forth evil things. 36.

But I tell you, on the day of judgment men will have to give account for every idle (inoperative, nonworking) word they speak. 37. For by your words you will be justified and acquitted, and by your words you will be condemned and sentenced.

Matthew 15:11 (AMPC) It is not what goes into the mouth of a man that makes him unclean and defiled, but what comes out of the mouth; this makes a man unclean and defiles [him].

Romans 10:9-10 (AMPC) 9. Because if you acknowledge and confess with your lips that Jesus is Lord and, in your heart, believe (adhere to, trust in, and rely on the truth) that God raised Him from the dead, you will be saved. 10. For with the heart a person believes (adheres to, trusts in, and relies on Christ) and so is justified (declared righteous, acceptable to God), and with the mouth he confesses (declares openly and speaks out freely his faith) and confirms [his] salvation.

Ephesians 4:29 (AMPC) Let no foul or polluting language, nor evil word nor unwholesome or worthless talk [ever] come out of your mouth, but only such [speech] as is good and beneficial to the spiritual progress of others, as is fitting to the need and the occasion, that it may be a blessing and give grace (God's favor) to those who hear it.

Ephesians 4:30 (AMPC) Let there be no filthiness (obscenity, indecency) nor foolish and sinful (silly and corrupt) talk, nor coarse jesting, which are not fitting or becoming; but instead voice your thankfulness [to God].

James 1:26 (AMPC) If anyone thinks himself to be religious (piously observant of the external duties of his faith) and does not bridle his tongue but deludes his own heart, this person's religious service is worthless (futile, barren).

James 3:10 (AMPC) Out of the same mouth come forth blessing and cursing. These things, my brethren, ought not to be so.

Of course, there are more, and I encourage you to look for yourself, dive into the Word of God and see what it says! I was thinking about this power that we have, and how it is so easy to let circumstances dictate us. How about speaking the opposite of what the normal reaction might be when a feeling hits us? Example: instead of saying "I am never going to get this task accomplished, I am not smart enough" say "I can do all things through Christ who strengthens me! Holy Spirit inside me is leading me and directing me!"

Jeremiah 33:3 (AMPC) Call to Me and I will answer you and show you great and mighty things, fenced in and hidden, which you do not know (do not distinguish and recognize, have knowledge of and understand).

Proverbs 8:12 (KJV) I wisdom dwell with prudence and find out knowledge of witty inventions.

There are so many promises that we have not even realized! We don't have to live depressed, discouraged, anxious, bitter, or afraid! I know that at times, this may not be easy, situations in your life may not have always been great.

There are a lot of stories out there of abuse, abandonment, betrayal, any number of situations that may have occurred. I probably couldn't even begin to list all of them, there is no way, but I just encourage you to step outside of your old way of thinking and start using the tools that God has given you.

Will it be overnight? No, probably not, and that is okay, but one step at a time, one word at a time, can start tearing down the walls that have been built around you. To start renewing your mind. Remember what Romans 12 says:

Romans 12:2 (AMPC) Do not be conformed to this world (this age), [fashioned after and adapted to its external, superficial customs], but be transformed (changed) by the [entire] renewal of your mind [by its new ideals and its new attitude], so that you may prove [for yourselves] what is the good and acceptable and perfect will of God, even the thing which is good and acceptable and perfect [in His sight for you].

On this journey, as you are learning a new behavior, remember that every day is a brand-new opportunity! As a "new creation" you honestly do not have to allow the things that happened or is currently happening, to affect your new life in Christ.

2 Corinthians 5:17 (AMPC) Therefore if any person is [ingrafted] in Christ (the Messiah) he is a new creation (a new creature altogether); the old [previous moral and spiritual condition] has passed away. Behold, the fresh and new has come!

You have power! It starts with your mouth! What are you creating with your words? What do you want to create? I was thinking about this "creative" thing and I was reminded that we are made in the exact image of God. Remember the book of Genesis? When God created man, he also gave him the ability to be creative himself.

Genesis 1:26-28 (AMPC) 26. God said, Let Us [Father, Son, and Holy Spirit] make mankind in Our image, after Our likeness, and let them have complete authority over the fish of the sea, the birds of the air, the [tame] beasts, and over all of the earth, and over everything that creeps upon the earth. 27. So God

created man in His own image, in the
image and likeness of God He created
him; male and female He created them
28. And God blessed them and said to
them, Be fruitful, multiply, and fill the
earth, and subdue it [using all its vast
resources in the service of God and man];
and have dominion over the fish of the
sea, the birds of the air, and over every
living creature that moves upon the earth.

It continues on stating that man not only had complete
dominion but also named everything. How? With what He
spoke! Imagine!

Gen 2:19-20 (AMPC) 19. And out of
the ground the Lord God formed every
[wild] beast and living creature of the
field and every bird of the air and brought
them to Adam to see what he would call
them; and whatever Adam called every
living creature, that was its name. 20.
And Adam gave names to all the livestock
and to the birds of the air and to every
[wild] beast of the field.

This is crazy! With just a word and it was, just like in
the very beginning God said a thing and boom, there it was!
And there it is.

Mark 11:23 (AMPC) Truly I tell you,
whoever says to this mountain, be lifted
up and thrown into the sea! And does

not doubt at all in his heart but believes
that what he says will take place, it will be
done for Him.

Jesus is telling us the same thing in the New Testament. He was confirming the original intent that we see in Genesis! What are you saying to your mountain? The scripture shows us so much. We just have to be willing to accept it as TRUTH! When Adam sinned way back when, there is no scripture that tells us that the dominion was taken away from him, the world was not suddenly handed over to Satan, this frame of thinking is incorrect. So, therefore, man still has dominion and still has power.

The power of "positive thinking" and "positive speech" is so relevant to our lives today! It is a productive tool used in therapy, self-help classes, psychology, doctors even promote this. The world is actually using biblical principles and does not even realize it. The Word of God works!

When we start realizing this as our reality, our lives will be changed dramatically. You are what you speak, you have what you say, you are creating your destiny with every syllable that comes out of your mouth. You are affecting those around you with your speech. You are choosing to be blessed or not to be blessed. This is such an incredible realization! So, start speaking to that mountain and stand back and watch it move!

CHAPTER 9

Where is your focus?

The question is about focus. How easy is it to get caught up in what is happening around you to the point of not being able to focus on anything else but that particular thing?

All too often we allow the worries of life to overwhelm us, to overwhelm our thoughts and cloud our vision. When we focus on the frustrations of the day or the uncertainties of tomorrow, we rob ourselves of peace in the present moment. So, what is the answer? Is there really a solution? I say yes, there is! You need to examine yourself. What has your attention? In order to get rid of the dark, we need to focus on the light. Fear needs to be replaced with faith; thoughts of illness need to be replaced with thoughts of health. Sound simple? Not always. It is a matter of retraining your thought life. You can never stop thinking, you can only direct your thinking, or in some cases, redirect your thinking. Interrupt your negative thoughts and replace them with the imagination of what you do want, stop being fixated on the negative aspects of what you don't want.

What are you empowering by your focus? Whatever we focus on, we give power to and whatever we focus on will grow. It is so easy to over think a thing. I don't know how many times I have wished that my brain would just shut-up for a minute, you know what I mean? I can be in the middle of a situation and it is so time consuming, so overwhelming, so emotionally draining, that it is so easy to just let my thoughts run wild with the what-ifs, the unknown ending of the situation can really be terrifying if we don't get a hold of ourselves, you know, just get it together, as it were.

We need to learn more about that peace that is actually available, because of Holy Spirit. It is in there, inside of us somewhere, but sometimes it can prove to be difficult to just "let go and let God," as the old saying goes. The battle that goes on in our minds is a real struggle, it can totally dictate how our entire day pans out, our entire lives pan out.

Dealing with stress, depression, and anxiety has turned into a multi-million-dollar business out there. Doctors and pharmaceutical companies are definitely making a buck when it comes to treating this problem. Now we are not knocking medication or going to see a physician by any means, thank the Lord that these avenues exist, but when it comes to everyday life, how can we make a change in how we react to a situation? It goes back to renewing your mind, with the help of Holy Spirit!

> Romans 12:2 (AMPC) Do not be conformed to this world (this age), [fashioned after and adapted to its external, superficial customs], but be transformed (changed) by the [entire] renewal of your mind [by its new ideals and its new attitude], so that you may prove [for yourselves] what is the good and acceptable and perfect will of God, even the thing

which is good and acceptable and perfect
[in His sight for you].

First you need to figure out what you are focusing on. What has your attention, what is it that is distracting you?

> Hebrews 12:2 (AMPC) Looking away
> [from all that will distract] to Jesus, who
> is the leader and the Source of our faith
> [giving the first incentive for our belief]
> and is also its Finisher [bringing it to
> maturity and perfection]. He, for the
> joy [of obtaining the prize] that was set
> before Him, endured the cross, despis-
> ing and ignoring the shame, and is now
> seated at the right hand of the throne of
> God.

Many of us have been in situations that completely overwhelmed us, whether it be caring for an ill loved one, dealing with a job loss, not knowing how the bills will get paid. Maybe you are dealing with a bad report from a doctor. I am sure that you can add to this list and it can seem never ending at times.

You may be wondering, Peace? What peace? How? Where is this peace that people keep referring to? I am a stressed mess! Sound familiar? Not being able to predict how or when a situation may turn around can be completely stressful, the fear of the unknown loves to creep in. But only if we let it. What are you allowing to dominate your emotions?

> John 14:27 (AMPC) Peace I leave with
> you; My [own] peace I now give and

bequeath to you. Not as the world gives do I give to you. Do not let your hearts be troubled, neither let them be afraid. [Stop allowing yourselves to be agitated and disturbed; and do not permit yourselves to be fearful and intimidated and cowardly and unsettled.]

Here this scripture is referring to that peace that we so often find ourselves lacking. Jesus assures us that He indeed has already given us peace, His own peace. Can you imagine, the kind of peace that Jesus has, He gave to you and me? It goes back to the realization that we have control of our thoughts and emotions. The enemy loves to try to convince us that he has the upper hand when things go awry in our lives, but he is a liar!

1 Peter 5:8-9 (AMPC) 8. Be well balanced (temperate, sober of mind), be vigilant and cautious at all times; for that enemy of yours, the devil, roams around like a lion roaring [in fierce hunger], seeking someone to seize upon and devour. 9. Withstand him; be firm in faith [against his onset—rooted, established, strong, immovable, and determined].

The devil roams around pretending to be a roaring lion because the only power he really has is by trying to throw thoughts at you, he can only have the upper hand if you allow it. This is where standing firm in our faith makes all the difference in the world!

Remember that the enemy comes to try to steal that peace that Jesus died for you to possess!

> John 10:10 (AMPC) The thief comes only in order to steal and kill and destroy. I came that they may have and enjoy life, and have it in abundance (to the full, till it overflows).

I love that old saying that it confuses the enemy when you are praising God in the midst of your circumstance! This is true. It confuses everyone when you are "going through" a situation and you still have a smile on your face and a genuine sense of peace and are remaining in a state of calmness in the middle of a storm. We have a perfect example of this in Jesus.

> Mark 4:35-41 (KJV) 35. And the same day, when the even was come, He saith unto them, 'Let us pass over unto the other side. 36. And when they had sent away the multitude, they took Him even as He was in the ship. And there were also with Him other little ships. 37. And there arose a great storm of wind, and the waves beat into the ship, so that it was now full. 38. And He was in the hinder part of the ship, asleep on a pillow: and they awake Him, and say unto Him, Master, carest thou not that we perish? 39. And he arose, and rebuked the wind, and said unto the sea, Peace, be still. And the wind ceased, and there was a great

calm. 40. And He said unto them, 'Why are ye so fearful? how is it that ye have no faith?' 41. And they feared exceedingly, and said one to another, 'What manner of man is this, that even the wind and the sea obey Him?'

Incredible! Right in the middle of a storm and Jesus was asleep on a pillow. Everyone freaking out, not understanding how He could rest so peacefully during what they thought was going to be the end of life as they knew it. And what did Jesus do? He spoke to the "situation" and commanded it to be still!

What are we speaking? What are we saying about what is going on? Remember that there is power in your tongue! I know that it is easy to "forget" sometimes that we *do* have power, we *do* have peace, but how easy is it to get "covered up" by life happening? A lot of things happen in life that perhaps we do not understand, we do not understand how this could have happened or why this has happened or how it will ever change. This is where that peace that passes understanding can rise up, when we give up our right to understand.

Proverbs 3:5-6 (AMPC) 5. Lean on, trust in, and be confident in the Lord with all your heart and mind and do not rely on your own insight or understanding. 6. In all your ways know, recognize, and acknowledge Him, and He will direct and make straight and plain your paths.

Philippians 4:7 (AMPC) And God's peace [shall be yours, that tranquil state of a soul assured of its salvation through Christ, and so fearing nothing from God and being content with its earthly lot of whatever sort that is, that peace] which transcends all understanding shall garrison and mount guard over your hearts and minds in Christ Jesus.

Things happen in life that we sure don't understand or expect, but the Peace that Jesus promised us is available! If... This is a big one... If we keep our eyes on Him!

Isaiah 26:3-4 (AMPC) 3. You will guard him and keep him in perfect and constant peace whose mind [both its inclination and its character] is stayed on You, because he commits himself to You, leans on You, and hopes confidently in You. 4. So trust in the Lord (commit yourself to Him, lean on Him, hope confidently in Him) forever; for the Lord God is an everlasting Rock [the Rock of Ages].

Keeping your mind, your thoughts on Jesus at all times, regardless of what is going on in life. The enemy would love to make you believe that whatever you are facing is bigger than the promises of God!

2 Corinthians 10:3-5 (KJV) 3. For though we walk in the flesh, we do not war after the flesh: 4. (For the weapons of our warfare are not carnal, but mighty through God to the pulling down of

strong holds;) 5. Casting down imagina-
tions, and every high thing that exalteth
itself against the knowledge of God and
bringing into captivity every thought to
the obedience of Christ;

It all goes back to your focus! It is hard to feel anxious
and discouraged when your focus is on Jesus and all of His
Glory! Our goal here is to have a glad heart regardless of what
is going on!

Proverbs 15:15 (AMPC) All the days of
the desponding and afflicted are made evil
[by anxious thoughts and forebodings],
but he who has a glad heart has a continual feast [regardless of circumstances].

Is this easy? Not all the time. It is a matter of training
our thought life to respond more to what Jesus says rather
than what our mind is thinking. Sound impossible? Not so!
We have so many promises! We just have to choose to believe!

Luke 1:37 (AMPC) For with God nothing is ever impossible and no word from
God shall be without power or impossible of fulfillment.

Jonah 2:7 (AMPC) When my soul
fainted upon me [crushing me], I earnestly and seriously remembered the
Lord; and my prayer came to You, into
Your holy temple.

We need to remember that God is always on our side. He is always there, always available! We can cast all of our cares, no matter how big or small, onto Him!

> 1 Peter 5:7 (AMPC) Casting the whole of your care [all your anxieties, all your worries, all your concerns, once and for all] on Him, for He cares for you affectionately and cares about you watchfully.

> Psalms 55:22 (AMPC) Cast your burden on the Lord [releasing the weight of it] and He will sustain you; He will never allow the [consistently] righteous to be moved (made to slip, fall, or fail).

We have to make a decision to not let fear control us. We must always rely on God, keeping our eyes on the things that are above and by choosing to focus on Him.

> Psalms 56:3-4 (AMPC) 3. What time I am afraid, I will have confidence in and put my trust and reliance in You. 4. By [the help of] God I will praise His word; on God I lean, rely, and confidently put my trust; I will not fear.

> Colossians 3:1-2 (AMPC) 1. IF THEN you have been raised with Christ [to a new life, thus sharing His resurrection from the dead], aim at and seek the [rich, eternal treasures] that are above, where Christ is, seated at the right hand of God.

2. And set your minds and keep them set
on what is above (the higher things), not
on the things that are on the earth.

In this relationship with Christ, we are continually learning how to function in a new manner, we are learning how to live a fuller, happier life. We are learning to readjust our focus when it is so easy to become overwhelmed with situations and circumstances. We are learning that by looking away from the things that can be distracting and keeping our minds set on the things that are above, by shifting our attention onto Jesus, because with Him we are now realizing that the fear of the unknown is a tactic that the enemy will try to use if we let him.

The enemy wants to cloud your vision and emotions with all of the worst case scenarios, the what-ifs, etc. in order to make you forget what the Lord has promised. He wants to steal your peace and joy. Remember that the joy of the Lord is your strength! Remember the promises of God, have Him remind you of His promises! He will, according to the scripture in Isaiah.

Isaiah 43:26 (AMPC) Put Me in remembrance [remind Me of your merits].

Isaiah 1:18 (AMPC) Come now, and let us reason together, says the Lord.

This is also where Holy Spirit helps, He reminds us of what God has said! Remember one of the roles of Holy Spirit is to bring comfort. Holy Spirit will always guide us back to the Father! Sometimes we may feel inadequate, but we have empowering strength because of Jesus Christ!

Philippians 4:13 (AMPC) I have strength for all things in Christ Who empowers me [I am ready for anything and equal to anything through Him Who infuses inner strength into me; I am self-sufficient in Christ's sufficiency].

Proverbs 4:25-27 (AMPC) 25. Let your eyes look right on [with fixed purpose], and let your gaze be straight before you. 26. Consider well the path of your feet and let all your ways be established and ordered aright. 27. Turn not aside to the right hand or to the left.

Isaiah 43:2-5 (AMPC) 2. When you pass through the waters, I will be with you, and through the rivers, they will not overwhelm you. When you walk through the fire, you will not be burned or scorched, nor will the flame kindle upon you. 3(a) For I am the Lord your God, the Holy one of Israel, your Savior; 4(a) Because you are precious in My sight and honored, and because I love you... 5. Fear not, for I am with you;

It is amazing when we finally realize that He is bigger than! If we are in the habit of continually shifting our focus onto the things that are above, to Him, keeping our eyes on Him instead of what is going on here, we realize that we can be, we are, above and not beneath, we are blessed, we are the head and not the tail! Just continue to listen to the voice of the Lord and *not* the voice of the enemy!

> Deuteronomy 28:1-13 (AMPC) 1. IF YOU will listen diligently to the voice of the Lord your God, being watchful to do all His commandments which I command you this day, the Lord your God will set you high above all the nations of the earth. 2. And all these blessings shall come upon you and overtake you if you heed the voice of the Lord your God. 3. Blessed shall you be in the city and blessed shall you be in the field. 4. Blessed shall be the fruit of your body and the fruit of your ground and the fruit of your beasts, the increase of your cattle and the young of your flock. 5. Blessed shall be your basket and your kneading trough. 6. Blessed shall you be when you come in and blessed shall you be when you go out. 7. The Lord shall cause your enemies who rise up against you to be defeated before your face; they shall come out against you one way and flee before you seven ways. 8. The Lord shall command the blessing upon you in your storehouse and in all that you undertake. And He will bless you in the land which the Lord your God gives you. 9. The Lord will establish you as a people holy to Himself, as He has sworn to you, if you keep the commandments of

the Lord your God and walk in His ways. 10. And all people of the earth shall see that you are called by the name [and in the presence of] the Lord, and they shall be afraid of you. 11. And the Lord shall make you have a surplus of prosperity, through the fruit of your body, of your livestock, and of your ground, in the land which the Lord swore to your fathers to give you. 12. The Lord shall open to you His good treasury, the heavens, to give the rain of your land in its season and to bless all the work of your hands; and you shall lend to many nations, but you shall not borrow. 13. And the Lord shall make you the head, and not the tail; and you shall be above only, and you shall not be beneath, if you heed the commandments of the Lord your God which I command you this day and are watchful to do them.

Amen! What a Mighty God we serve!

CHAPTER 10

Making the Word Final Authority

Malachi 3:6 (AMPC) For I am the Lord, I do not change;

Isaiah 40:8 (AMPC) The grass withers, the flower fades, but the word of our God will stand forever.

Psalms 9:10 (AMPC) And they who know Your name [who have experience and acquaintance with Your mercy] will lean on and confidently put their trust in You, for You, Lord, have not forsaken those who seek (inquire of and for) You [on the authority of God's Word and the right of their necessity].

Isaiah 66:2 (AMPC) For all these things My hand has made, and so all these things have come into being [by and for

Me], says the Lord. But this is the man
to whom I will look and have regard:
he who is humble and of a broken or
wounded spirit, and who trembles at My
word and reveres My commands.

Psalms 119:89 (AMPC) Forever, O Lord,
Your word is settled in heaven [stands
firm as the heavens].

What does it mean to make the Word final authority?

It means believing what God says instead of believing
everything else. Despite what your circumstances say, not
letting them dictate your emotions, dictate the way that you
spend your time, dictate your mood, dictate your level of
peace and joy. We know that living life led by our feelings can
keep us in a state of unpredictability and uncertainty which
inevitably can lead to depression and anxiety. The beauty of
God's Word is that God has no double standard. He is the
same yesterday, today, and forever. He is always stable; He has
always been stable and will always be stable. His Word gives
you stability when everything else around you gives way.

Matthew 7:24-29 (AMPC) 24. So everyone who hears these words of Mine and
acts upon them [obeying them] will be
like a sensible (prudent, practical, wise)
man who built his house upon the rock.
25. And the rain fell and the floods came
and the winds blew and beat against
that house; yet it did not fall, because it
had been founded on the rock. 26. And
everyone who hears these words of Mine

and does not do them will be like a stu-
pid (foolish) man who built his house
upon the sand. 27. And the rain fell and
the floods came and the winds blew and
beat against that house, and it fell—and
great and complete was the fall of it. 28.
When Jesus had finished these sayings
[the Sermon on the Mount], the crowds
were astonished and overwhelmed with
bewildered wonder at His teaching, 29.
For He was teaching as one Who had
[and was] authority.

This parable teaches us that if you have a solid foundation, when circumstances arise, you will not be shaken! If
you let His word and what He says settle the issues of life,
you will be confident, when everyone else around you is in a
state of confusion, you will have peace. When everyone else
is coming unhinged, you can be an overcomer!

Is this an easy process? Not necessarily, it actually takes
digging into His Word, getting to know what He says, getting to know the scriptures, and falling back on the Word to
combat anything that the enemy throws at you, or that life in
general may throw at you.

John 16:33 (AMPC) I have told you
these things, so that in Me you may have
[perfect] peace and confidence. In the
world you have tribulation and trials and
distress and frustration; but be of good
cheer [take courage; be confident, certain, undaunted]! For I have overcome
the world. [I have deprived it of power

to harm you and have conquered it for you.]

The Lord is telling us here that He has overcome for us! It is already done! This is incredible news! So why do we get so flustered and upset? We can insert this scripture:

> John 10:10 (AMPC) The thief comes only in order to steal and kill and destroy. I came that they may have and enjoy life, and have it in abundance (to the full, till it overflows).

We are using this very familiar passage of course, but it serves as a stark reminder that the enemy wants to rob you of your peace and joy. If he can keep you in a state of upheaval and keep you all stressed out, he knows that you will probably not be ready to worship God in the midst of it. His goal is to keep you distracted and keep your focus off of God. He loves to throw distractions at people, *but God!* He tells us in the same scripture that He came so that you can have and enjoy life! A lot of people are living life, yeah, but they certainly do not seem to be enjoying it. But we have been given the key! The Word of God is our key!

We always look to Jesus as our example, how He handled situations and His response to the enemy.

> Matthew 4:2-11 (AMPC) 2. And He went without food for forty days and forty nights, and later He was hungry. 3. And the tempter came and said to Him, If You are God's Son, command these stones to be made [loaves of] bread. 4.

But He replied, It has been written, Man shall not live and be upheld and sustained by bread alone, but by every word that comes forth from the mouth of God. 5. Then the devil took Him into the holy city and placed Him on a turret (pinnacle, gable) of the temple sanctuary. 6. And he said to Him, If You are the Son of God, throw Yourself down; for it is written, He will give His angels charge over you, and they will bear you up on their hands, lest you strike your foot against a stone. 7. Jesus said to him, On the other hand, it is written also, You shall not tempt, test thoroughly, or try exceedingly the Lord your God. 8. Again, the devil took Him up on a very high mountain and showed Him all the kingdoms of the world and the glory (the splendor, magnificence, pre-eminence, and excellence) of them. 9. And he said to Him, 'These things, all taken together, I will give You, if You will prostrate Yourself before me and do homage and worship me.' 10. Then Jesus said to him, 'Be gone, Satan! For it has been written, you shall worship the Lord your God, and Him alone shall you serve.' 11. Then the devil departed from Him, and behold, angels came and ministered to Him.

We see here that Jesus always responded with The Word of God! Jesus is our example of how to respond! Any situation can be combated with the Word! The Word is our weapon. It is so easy to get caught up in our emotions, especially when you feel like there is nothing that you can do to change the situation, when you feel hopeless and discouraged, this is when we learn to lean on Him!

> Proverbs 3:5-6 (AMPC) 5. Lean on, trust in, and be confident in the Lord with all your heart and mind and do not rely on your own insight or understanding. 6. In all your ways know, recognize, and acknowledge Him, and He will direct and make straight and plain your paths.

Remember, looking away from the distraction and keeping your eyes on things that are above.

> Philippians 4:8 (AMPC) For the rest, brethren, whatever is true, whatever is worthy of reverence and is honorable and seemly, whatever is just, whatever is pure, whatever is lovely and lovable, whatever is kind and winsome and gracious, if there is any virtue and excellence, if there is anything worthy of praise, think on and weigh and take account of these things [fix your minds on them].

What is worthy of Praise? Only Jesus! He is our truth; He is just and pure and lovely and excellent! *He* is our way when we don't know how to navigate through life!

John 14:6 (AMPC) Jesus said to him, 'I
am the Way and the Truth and the Life.'

You have to make a decision to live by faith and not by
sight. Make a decision to commit yourself to the authority
of His Word and then there won't be anything in this unsta-
ble world that could possibly steal that security from you! It
goes back to your focus; you have to decide that you are not
going to focus on the negatives, but you are going to focus on
Jesus! Remember where your attention goes, your emotions
will follow.

There are so many promises in the Word of God. I
encourage you to not take this subject lightly. You have to
make the decision that the Word is what you are always going
to rely on regardless of the circumstance, regardless of your
feelings. This is where Holy Spirit comes in and reminds you
of God's promises!

John 14:26-27 (AMPC) 26. But
the Comforter (Counselor, Helper,
Intercessor, Advocate, Strengthener,
Standby), the Holy Spirit, Whom the
Father will send in My name [in My place,
to represent Me and act on My behalf],
He will teach you all things. And He will
cause you to recall (will remind you of,
bring to your remembrance) everything I
have told you. 27. Peace I leave with you;
My [own] peace I now give and bequeath
to you. Not as the world gives do I give to
you. Do not let your hearts be troubled,
neither let them be afraid. [Stop allowing
yourselves to be agitated and disturbed;

and do not permit yourselves to be fearful and intimidated and cowardly and unsettled.]

I love the last part of verse 27 where He tells us to stop allowing ourselves to be agitated and disturbed; and do not permit ourselves to be fearful and intimidated and cowardly and unsettled. This sounds just like we have a choice! I want to choose to *not* be agitated, disturbed, troubled, afraid, intimidated, and unsettled! How about you? I choose peace! I am ready to rise up!

> Isa 60:1 (AMPC) ARISE [from the depression and prostration in which circumstances have kept you—rise to a new life]! Shine (be radiant with the glory of the Lord), for your light has come, and the glory of the Lord has risen upon you!

This new life is accessible! Why? How? Because we know now that we have a choice!

> Deuteronomy 30:19-20 (AMPC) 19. I call heaven and earth to witness this day against you that I have set before you life and death, the blessings and the curses; therefore, choose life, that you and your descendants may live 20. And may love the Lord your God, obey His voice, and cling to Him. For He is your life and the length of your days, that you may dwell in the land which the Lord swore to give

to your fathers, to Abraham, Isaac, and
Jacob.

Looking at the scriptures that we have been using so
far, these are all prime examples of what is available to us!
His promises are Yes and Amen! We just have to make the
decision to start living our lives the way that He intended for
us to live! It is possible!

In this new understanding of who we are, who *He* is
and what He has done for us; in this revelation we now know
what has been made available to us. Because of the sacrifice
of Jesus Christ and knowing that Holy Spirit dwells inside
of us, we have all that we need to succeed! We just have to
learn more about His Word, this is key. This is how we fight
every battle and win, by knowing how to respond to life's
situations. We want to replicate our way of living in the same
manner that Jesus did. He only did what He saw the Father
do, and only said what He heard the Father say.

> John 8:28 (AMPC) So Jesus added,
> 'When you have lifted up the Son of
> Man [on the cross], you will realize
> (know, understand) that I am He [for
> Whom you look] and that I do nothing
> of Myself (of My own accord or on My
> own authority), but I say [exactly] what
> My Father has taught Me.'

This is our ultimate goal, to be as much like Jesus as
possible!

Understanding that our foundation is the Word, it is in
exercising this "muscle" that it will get stronger and stronger.

Digging in and not letting everything and everyone dictate how you respond to life happening is the challenge here.

> Josh 1:8-9 (AMPC) 8. This Book of the Law shall not depart out of your mouth, but you shall meditate on it day and night, that you may observe and do according to all that is written in it. For then you shall make your way prosperous, and then you shall deal wisely and have good success. 9. Have not I commanded you? Be strong, vigorous, and very courageous. Be not afraid, neither be dismayed, for the Lord your God is with you wherever you go.

These scriptures challenge us to meditate on the Word day and night. We all want to be strong, vigorous and courageous. It is possible by seeking God through the Word, and letting that Word become our foundation, He is a rewarder to the ones who earnestly and diligently seek Him!

> Hebrews 11:6 (AMPC) But without faith it is impossible to please and be satisfactory to Him. For whoever would come near to God must [necessarily] believe that God exists and that He is the rewarder of those who earnestly and diligently seek Him [out].

> Joshua 23:6 (AMPC) So be very courageous and steadfast to keep and do all that is written in the Book of the Law of

Moses, turning not aside from it to the
right hand or the left.

Realizing that The Word of God is the only truth, the
one and only truth, makes us view the world differently,
view all situations and circumstances differently. Not being
swayed by everything we see, hear or think may be a foreign
concept to most people, but this decision to base our lives on
the Word and what God has to say will trump our natural
thinking every time. His Word will trump what our flesh is
trying to say to us, what the world would have us believe,
even what our friends or sometimes family members may be
saying regarding our current situation.

The Word teaches us that even though feelings come
and go, fads come and go, belief systems come and go, God's
Word will always remain. He is the same yesterday, today, and
forever. His Word will never change, no matter how many
times we hear a message contrary to this. It does not matter
that this is a new era, a new generation with new ideas, it is
not okay to compromise on the Truth of God's Word. His
Word will still be standing, still be solid, when everything
else is falling apart.

We need to take our thought life captive. Casting away
anything that is contrary to what we know that the Word
says.

2 Corinthians 10:5 (AMPC) [Inasmuch
as we] refute arguments and theories and
reasonings and every proud and lofty
thing that sets itself up against the [true]
knowledge of God; and we lead every
thought and purpose away captive into

the obedience of Christ (the Messiah, the Anointed one).

John 12:44-50 (AMPC) 44. But Jesus loudly declared, 'The one who believes in Me does not [only] believe in and trust in and rely on Me, but [in believing in Me he believes] in Him Who sent Me. 45. And whoever sees Me sees Him Who sent Me. 46. I have come as a Light into the world, so that whoever believes in Me [whoever cleaves to and trusts in and relies on Me] may not continue to live in darkness. 47. If anyone hears My teachings and fails to observe them [does not keep them, but disregards them], it is not I who judges him. For I have not come to judge and to condemn and to pass sentence and to inflict penalty on the world, but to save the world. 48. Anyone who rejects Me and persistently sets Me at naught, refusing to accept My teachings, has his judge [however]; for the [very] message that I have spoken will itself judge and convict him at the last day. 49. This is because I have never spoken on My own authority or of My own accord or as self-appointed, but the Father Who sent Me has Himself given Me orders [concerning] what to say and what to tell. 50. And I know that His commandment is (means) eternal life. So, whatever I speak, I am saying [exactly] what My Father has

told Me to say and in accordance with
His instructions.'

Jesus came as a Light to this world, He came to share the Word, to teach us and guide us so that we can come out of the darkness, come out of living a life full of guilt and shame and hopelessness, and step into a brand-new reality, a brand-new way of thinking, a brand-new life. The Word is full of promises, full of hope, full of life, and this is all for you. Regardless of what is happening right now, regardless of what has happened in the past, if you make the Word the Final Authority in your life, you will begin to see things in a whole new light! I am so excited for you to start this journey and everyday discover more and more of the promises, more and more of what is available to you through this relationship with Jesus Christ who *is* the Word!

> Luke 1:37 (AMPC) For with God nothing is ever impossible and no word from God shall be without power or impossible of fulfillment. Amen!

FINAL THOUGHTS

In conclusion, I hope that this has started to make a difference in your life. My goal was to touch on some of the topics that I felt were relevant in the everyday life of the everyday person. I know that the topics were and still are relevant in my own life. At times, it may be a challenge to remember who you really are according to the Word of God. Sometimes we all need to be reminded by going back to the Word for a reality check. Even though I am on this journey to help spread the Word of God, there are times when I personally need a little refresher course, we all do! It is incredible how going back to review His promises for us can make the day brighter. Oh, the goodness of His love. It is such an incredible thing!

Circumstances may tap you on the shoulder trying to demand your attention, but when you decide to look to Jesus and let Him be bigger, then you will find your peace, find a better way to get through the day. Realizing that the circumstance is not bigger than God! His Word is packed with promise!

You can claim the promises and re-establish your identity in Him. Casting all of your cares onto Him and looking away from all of the distractions in life and focusing on the One who holds your future, the One who holds your peace! Once you realize that you were created By Him and for Him, that He longs for a relationship with you, when you have that great moment of encounter with Jesus Christ that changes your life in such a dramatic way that you can no longer continue in the previous way that you were living your life. When you discover that there is so much more!

> Titus 3:5-7 (AMPC) 5. He saved us, not because of any works of righteousness that we had done, but because of His own pity and mercy, by [the] cleansing [bath] of the new birth (regeneration) and renewing of the Holy Spirit, 6. Which He poured out [so] richly upon us through Jesus Christ our Savior. 7.[And He did it in order] that we might be justified by His grace (by His favor, wholly undeserved), [that we might be acknowledged and counted as conformed to the divine will in purpose, thought, and action], and that we might become heirs of eternal life according to [our] hope.

His incredible love for us is absolutely mind blowing! My encouragement to you is to spend time with Him, not only in the Word, but by spending time with Him, building the relationship into something so personal that when people see you, they see Christ in you.

> 2 Corinthians 3:18 (AMPC) And all of us, as with unveiled face, [because we] continued to behold [in the Word of God] as in a mirror the glory of the Lord,

are constantly being transfigured into His very own image in ever increasing splendor and from one degree of glory to another; [for this comes] from the Lord [Who is] the Spirit.

When we learn to focus on the things that are above, our emotions will follow the focus, and what better thing to focus on than the Higher Kingdom and all that it contains!

Matthew 6:21 (AMPC) For where your treasure is, there will your heart be also.

Matthew 6:33 (AMPC) But seek (aim at and strive after) first of all His kingdom and His righteousness (His way of doing and being right), and then all these things taken together will be given you besides.

Psalms 123:1 (AMPC) UNTO YOU do I lift up my eyes, O You Who are enthroned in heaven.

Make the decision today to keep your focus on the Lord, when you are looking at Him, everything else will pale in comparison!

Psalms 121 (NKJV) 1. I will lift up my eyes to the hills—From whence comes my help? 2. My help comes from the LORD, Who made heaven and earth. 3. He will not allow your foot to be moved; He who keeps you will not slumber. 4. Behold, He who keeps Israel Shall neither slumber nor sleep. 5. The LORD is your keeper; The LORD is your shade at your right hand. 6. The sun shall not strike you by day, Nor the moon by night. 7. The LORD shall preserve you from all evil; He shall preserve your soul. 8 The LORD shall preserve your going out and your coming in. From this time forth, and even forevermore.

ABOUT THE AUTHOR

....

Beth Schreiber is an author, recording artist, and sought-after conference speaker. She is an ordained Pastor and co-founder of Open Heaven Worship Ministries, a thriving Apostolic and Prophetic Ministry that raises up and oversees ministries for the work of the Kingdom.

Beth grew up as a Pastor's daughter in a small town in Kentucky. She started singing at a very young age in church and eventually started traveling throughout the region, ministering the Word of God and singing as a solo artist. Her life took a radical shift when she married Apostle Matt Schreiber. God spoke to Beth that her life and season in Kentucky were coming to an end and that He had new things on the horizon for her. With that word from God in her heart, she sold everything and moved to the Northwest to begin a new life and ministry for God.

Beth is an anointed Psalmist and Minister. She is a published song writer, a member of BMI and has a southern gospel music CD called "Pressing On" and her self-published book *The Power Lies Within You* brings encouragement to others through the word of her testimony.

CPSIA information can be obtained
at www.ICGtesting.com
Printed in the USA
LVHW091736140521
687463LV00004B/148